IT'S A BREEZE

42 LIVELY ENGLISH LESSONS ON AMERICAN IDIOMS

BY TONI ABERSON

EDITED BY ERIC H. ROTH

Published by
Chimayo Press

It's A Breeze
42 Lively English Lessons on American Idioms

Copyright © 2013 Toni Aberson

Aberson, Toni.
It's A Breeze : 42 lively English lessons on American idioms / by Toni Aberson ; edited by Eric H. Roth.
p. cm.
Includes index.

LCCN 2012944362
ISBN 978-1-4810354-2-2
eISBN 978-0-9847985-2-0

1. English language—Conversation and phrase books.
2. Americanisms. 3. Idioms. I. Roth, Eric Hermann, 1961-
II. Title. III. Title: 42 lively English lessons on American idioms. IV. Title: Forty-two lively English lessons on American idioms.

PE1131.A24 2012   428.3'4
                         QBI12-600201

Photographs by Toni Aberson, Dani Roth, Maya Roth, and Laurie Selik. Additional photographs from iStockphoto.com.

Book design by Stacey Aaronson
www.creative-collaborations.com

To order additional copies, share comments, ask questions, or contribute American idioms, please visit www.ChimayoPress.com or email eric@compellingconversations.com

Chimayo Press
3766 Redwood Ave., Los Angeles, CA 90066-3506
United States of America

1-855-ESL-Book or 1-855-375-2665
(toll-free in United States and Canada)

www.ChimayoPress.com

Dedicated to Lisa Aberson (1947-2007)

Lisa lived with strength and gusto.
She had a passion for words and an enthusiasm for life.
I miss her daily.

TABLE OF CONTENTS

INTRODUCTION

He's wet behind the ears.
The test was a piece of cake.
She came right out of the blue.

Do you know the words, but don't understand the meaning? These short sentences use common American idioms. You will find idioms on television, in sports, at work, and at school.

Idioms are also one reason English can be a difficult language for many adults to learn. You have to learn common American idioms to really speak English in a natural style.

The good news is that studying idioms – even as an intermediate English student - can also be fun. We will go at a comfortable pace, learning idiom by idiom. In fact, each short lesson is built around a single common American idiom and its meaning. You will read a brief story of daily life, learn some vocabulary, write a few sentences, and ask and answer some conversation questions. The lively lessons encourage thinking and sharing in a relaxed atmosphere. Groups of lessons have been organized together in seven units. The units go from easier to more difficult. You will get a chance to show your increased knowledge on unit quizzes too.

As you know, learning English is often the key to a better life today. These lessons will help you use more colorful English in your life. These lessons will also help you gain a better understanding of the English you hear around you and on television, learn more about American culture, and speak more like an American. Idiom by idiom, you will find speaking English less difficult and more fun. You might even find speaking English "a breeze."

Enjoy,

Toni Aberson
October 2012

UNIT ONE
LET'S GET STARTED!

Here are some easy lessons about idioms that are common in the United States. Doing these few warm-up lessons will help you **learn the ropes.** If learning about American culture is on your **bucket list,** you will enjoy these lessons. If you learn all the vocabulary in this book, you can **toot your own horn.** See how idioms work? Once you start using them, it is hard to stop. They are fun. They make writing and speaking more interesting. Let's get started! You will see. **It's a breeze.**

A person has to learn the ropes to sail a boat.

It's a breeze – it's easy; it's pleasant.

Learn the ropes – learn how to do the job.

Bucket list – a list of experiences you would like sometime in your life.

Toot your own horn – brag about how great you are.

1

IT'S A BREEZE

USAGE

Don't worry about the written driving test. **It's a breeze.**

MEANING

It's a breeze means it's easy and pleasant.

STORY

Jana had a new job, working as a cashier in the local grocery store. She was a little worried because she had never worked a cash register before.

The manager said, "There's no need to worry. An experienced cashier will work with you the first few days. She'll show you how to scan groceries and how to put groceries in a cloth sack or paper bag. If there's an unexpected problem, she'll take over. Trust me, **it's a breeze.**"

VOCABULARY

breeze – a slight, gentle wind.

✦ *The people on the beach enjoyed the breeze from the ocean.*

cashier – the person who totals the amount due, collects the payment from the customer, puts the money in the cash register, and gives appropriate change back to the customer.

✦ *Managers and customers value cashiers who are friendly.*

scan – using the bar code on the can or package that automatically feeds the price of the item into the cash register computer.

✦ *For some reason, the spaghetti package would not scan, so the cashier entered the code by hand.*

sack – a bag that is used to carry things.

✦ *A good cashier will put heavier items in the bottom of the sack, or grocery bag, so that lighter items are not broken or smashed.*

unexpected – not expected; unplanned; not anticipated.

✦ *I received an unexpected letter from an old school friend.*

PRACTICE

1. In the following sentences, fill in the blank with the vocabulary word that best matches the meaning of the sentence:

   A grocery _____ often has to stand on her feet for hours at a time.

   Be careful when you put the eggs in the _____.

   The pleasant _____ became a strong wind in just minutes.

2. Use each of the letters in the word groceries (G R O C E R I E S) as the first letter of something you could buy at a grocery store. You may work with a partner. Note the example with the letter G.

   G: grapes

   R: _____

   O: _____

   C: _____

   E: _____

   R: _____

   I: _____

   E: _____

   S: _____

CONVERSATION

1. Have you ever worried about something that later **was a breeze**? How did you feel beforehand? How did you feel afterward?

2. Have you ever had a job where you handled money? What was it? Have you ever worked a cash register? Was it easy? What was the hardest part of using a cash register?

3. Do you ever do the grocery shopping? Are there differences between shopping for groceries in America and shopping for groceries in your native country? What are the differences? Which do you prefer? Why?

Other choices: Instead of saying **It's a breeze**, one might say **it was a walk in the park.** Both sayings mean that the experience was easy and pleasant.

LEARN THE ROPES

USAGE

Whenever you start a new job, you have to **learn the ropes.**

MEANING

If you **learn the ropes,** you learn how to do the job. The meaning of this idiom started from learning how to sail a boat. Now it means learning how to do any job.

STORY

Steve got a job as a server at a popular Italian restaurant. He wanted to start waiting on tables his first night on the job to earn a salary and tips. The boss said, "Slow down. Don't rush into things. Work with Mario for a few days and see how we do things. First, you have to **learn the ropes.** Then we'll talk about your schedule."

VOCABULARY

ropes – long strands of fibers used for tying or binding.

✦ *Cowboys use ropes for many chores on the ranch.*

restaurant - a place where people buy meals and sit down for breakfast, lunch, or dinner.

✦ *The Indian restaurant had a good selection of vegetarian dishes.*

server – a waiter or waitress; a person who serves tables in a restaurant.

✦ *Since the server was so good, we left a big tip.*

salary – a set amount of money paid for a job every week or every two weeks.

✦ *A car salesman usually earns a salary plus commission.*

tips – extra money paid by customers to servers for their good service.

✦ *Waitresses who are cheerful and efficient earn good tips.*

PRACTICE

1. Fill in each blank with the vocabulary word that best expresses the meaning of the sentence.

If the server does not bring the food that was ordered, a customer may leave a smaller _____ than usual.

My grandmother seldom ate in a _____.

The boss said that if I stayed for six months and did a good job, my _____ could increase by as much as 10%.

2. List all the words used in this lesson that you did not know. Try to guess their meanings. Then, look in a dictionary for the definitions of the words you listed. Did you guess correctly?

_____   _____

_____   _____

_____   _____

CONVERSATION

Sometimes people have to **learn the ropes** at a new school.
Sometimes people have to **learn the ropes** at a new job.
Sometimes people have to **learn the ropes** in a new country.

1. Describe a situation in which you had to **learn the ropes**. Did anyone help you? How?

2. Describe a situation in which you helped someone else **learn the ropes**. Were you a patient teacher? Was your student a fast learner?

3

TOOT YOUR OWN HORN

USAGE

Muhammad Ali enjoyed **tooting his own horn.**

MEANING

A person who **toots his own horn** is bragging about himself. He is making noise about his abilities. At times, it is considered poor manners to **toot one's own horn.** In some situations, bragging about oneself is okay. In America, athletes and politicians often **toot their own horns.**

STORY

When the boxer Muhammad Ali first proclaimed, "I am the greatest," some people felt uncomfortable. They had been taught that people should not brag about themselves. He said, "I can fly like a butterfly, sting like a bee." He liked to play with words. He liked to tease. Now, when Ali **toots his own horn,** most people smile and enjoy his fun.

VOCABULARY

---

toot – to blow into a horn; the short, sharp sound of a horn.

+ *In some cities, it is illegal to toot a car horn for no reason.*

brag – boast about oneself; boast about someone closely related.

+ *When John hit the home run that won the game, his father bragged, "That's my son!"*

boxer – an athlete who fights according to set rules; a prizefighter.

+ *The boxer Manny Pacquiao is famous throughout the world.*

comfortable – at ease, relaxed.

+ *I am comfortable when I wear my old sweatshirt.*

uncomfortable – without ease; feeling awkward.

+ *The baby felt uncomfortable in her wet diaper.*

PRACTICE

---

1. Write a sentence using the idiom **toot your own horn** correctly.

_____

_____

2. Fill in the blanks in the following sentences with the vocabulary word that best suits the meaning of the sentence:

Joe Louis was a heavyweight champion _____.

When the heat is turned up too high, I feel _____.

When the traffic light changed from red to green, I heard a horn _____ from the car behind me.

CONVERSATION

1. Have you ever **tooted your own horn?** About what? How did others react?

2. Have you ever become upset when someone else **tooted his own horn?** Why? How did you feel?

3. Can you think of three situations in which it might help you to **toot your own horn?**

4

BUCKET LIST

USAGE

I want to visit Ireland before I **kick the bucket.**
A trip to Ireland is on my **bucket list.**

MEANING

The expression **kick the bucket** is a casual way to refer to death. If someone says, "I want to visit Ireland before I **kick the bucket,**" it means I want to visit Ireland at sometime in my life. From this idiom comes the term **bucket list.** A **bucket list** is a list of things you want to do before you **kick the bucket.** In other words, your **bucket list** would be a list of the experiences you want at sometime in your life.

STORY

Nancy and Sue were talking about their **bucket lists.** Nancy said, "I for sure want to visit New York and see the Statue of Liberty before I **kick the bucket.**"

Sue said, "I would rather visit Hawaii. My dream is to live there for a few years at some point in my life."

Nancy said, "That is a good one. I'm going to add spending at least a year in Hawaii to my **bucket list**."

VOCABULARY

bucket – a pail; a container with a handle for carrying water, soil, etc.

✦ *The farmer gave his thirsty horse a bucket of cold water.*

casual – informal; relaxed.

✦ *In our office, we can wear casual clothes to work on Friday.*

death – the end of life; the state of non-life.

✦ *The notice of the writer's death was in the newspaper.*

Statue of Liberty – a very large statue in New York Harbor that has been the symbol of liberty to many.

✦ *The tourist bus stopped so we could see the Statue of Liberty.*

dream – a hope for the future; a goal one wants to achieve.

✦ *My dream house would have a large garden with a waterfall.*

PRACTICE

1. Fill in each of the blanks in the following sentences with the appropriate vocabulary word.

   The _____ has been a symbol of freedom.

   My friends and I ate a _____ of chicken at our picnic.

   I _____ of the day when I will live in a new house.

2. Where do you definitely want to go sometime in your life? What do you definitely want to see sometime in your life? What do you definitely want to do sometime in your life? List at least three things that would be on your **bucket list**.

   _____

   _____

   _____

CONVERSATION

1. Discuss your **bucket list**. If there are items you do not want to share, you may keep them to yourself. Why is it a good idea to make a **bucket list**?

2. Do you have a dream for the future? What kind of house would you like to live in? Where would you like to live? Again, if there are some things you do not want to share, you may keep them to yourself.

UNIT TWO

FUN WITH FOOD

Many people grow food. Many people shop for food. Many people cook food. We all think about food, and we all talk about food. Food surrounds us with its wonderful smells and colorful appearance. Words about food also surround us.

It's fun. It's good. It's a piece of cake.

Because tastes in food are different from one country to another, expressions that refer to food are also different in each country. In the United States, common idioms include **couch potato** and **a piece of cake**. Do you know the meanings of these expressions? By the time you finish this unit, you will understand these expressions and many more. Enjoy your word feast!

5

A PIECE OF CAKE

USAGE

The math test was **a piece of cake**.

MEANING

The expression **a piece of cake** means very easy. If an action is **a piece of cake**, the person has no difficulties doing it.

STORY

Selena was worried about her upcoming interview for admission into the art school. What would the director ask her? How could she prepare? She decided to take her best drawings with her. But what if they weren't good enough? What if the director felt she had no talent? She hardly slept the night before the interview. Her mother tried to reassure her, but Selena remained very nervous. When Selena came home, her mother asked, "How did it go?"

Selena smiled happily and said, "It was **a piece of cake**. They were so kind! They really liked my work. I can start in the fall. All my worrying was for nothing."

VOCABULARY

upcoming – in the near future.

+ *The team that wins the upcoming basketball game will be the next state champions.*

interview – a conversation for a set purpose e.g. an interview for a job.

+ *It is important to dress appropriately for a job interview.*

difficulties – problems.

+ *My difficulties started when my luggage was lost.*

prepare – do work before an event so it will go more smoothly.

+ *Donna did a lot of running to prepare for the long marathon race.*

reassure – encourage; give confidence to.

+ *The coach reassured his team that they still had time to win the game.*

PRACTICE

1. Write down the vocabulary word that best fits the meaning of each sentence.

   I _____ most of the meal before my guests arrive.

   I was nervous about the _____ interview.

   I think the _____ went well.

2. List three actions that are **a piece of cake** for you.

   _____

   _____

   _____

CONVERSATION

1. Have you ever had the experience of being worried about something beforehand and then finding out it was really **a piece of cake**? What was your experience? What were you afraid it was going to be? How did you feel afterwards?

2. When you are worried about an upcoming experience, do you have any techniques you use to calm yourself? What are they?

Other choices: Another expression that means exactly the same as **a piece of cake** is **easy as pie.** One may say, "The exam was **a piece or cake**," or one may say, "The exam was **easy as pie**."

6

IN A PICKLE

USAGE

John missed his airplane, and now he is **in a pickle.**

MEANING

If a person is **in a pickle,** he is in a difficult situation. He is dealing with a tough problem. There is no easy answer to his problem.

STORY

Alex was a traveling salesman. He spent part of his time in Los Angeles and part in Houston. He wasn't married, but he had a girlfriend in Los Angeles and another girlfriend in Houston. He told each of the women that she was the only one for him. On his birthday, Alex was working in Los Angeles. His girlfriend from Houston went to Los Angeles to surprise him. The two women met, and now both are angry with him. Alex is **in a pickle.**

VOCABULARY

pickle – a cucumber that has been cured in vinegar and spices.

+ *I like a sour dill pickle on the side when I eat a hamburger.*

difficult – not easy; hard.

+ *Sarah thought the history test was difficult.*

traveling salesman – a person whose job requires him to travel to different places to sell his goods and services.

+ *A traveling salesman usually has a regular route that he follows.*

surprise – an unexpected happening.

+ *The movie had a surprise ending.*

angry – very upset.

+ *I became angry when I saw the man beat his dog.*

PRACTICE

1. Read the following sentences. Then fill in each of the blanks with the most appropriate vocabulary word.

   Arthur Miller's play *Death of a Salesman* is about the life of a
   _____ and his family.

When I am _____, I often cannot think straight.

A dill _____ is often served with a corned beef sandwich.

2. Read each of the following sentences. Does the sentence describe someone who is **in a pickle**? If the person described is **in a pickle**, circle yes. If the person is not **in a pickle**, circle no.

   John had a flat tire on the freeway, and he had no spare tire.
   Yes / No

   Susie got a surprise bonus check from her boss.
   Yes / No

   Bill earned all A's on his report card and made the Honor Roll.
   Yes / No

   Karla forgot her lines in the school play.
   Yes / No

Discuss your answers with your classmates.

CONVERSATION

1. Have any of your friends ever been **in a pickle**? What happened?

2. Can you think of a movie or a TV show when somebody was **in a pickle**? What happened?

3. Do you like pickles? Do you prefer sweet or sour pickles?

Other choices: There are many idioms for being in a difficult situation. You may say **in a jam** rather than **in a pickle**. You may also say **up a creek** or **up a creek without a paddle** rather than **in a pickle**.

7

A PEACH

USAGE

She is a peach!

MEANING

If you say a person is **a peach**, you mean that person is a rare and wonderful person. You value her highly. She is great. She is **a peach**.

STORY

John had two pets, a dog and a cat. When John broke his leg and was taken to the hospital, he worried about his animals. Who would feed them? Who would take his dog for walks? Who would play with them? His neighbor Mary said, "For goodness sake, John, don't worry. I'll take care of them as long as you need help. They know me, and they like me. We'll be fine. You just get well."

John said, "Mary, you're **a peach**. You are **a real peach**. What would I do without you? Thank you. Thank you."

VOCABULARY

---

peach – a round, juicy orange-pink fruit with a fuzzy skin.

   ✦ *My grandparents owned a peach farm in Georgia.*

rare – not often found; very good.

   ✦ *White tigers are very rare and an endangered species.*

wonderful – very good; marvelous.

   ✦ *Bob had a wonderful time at the party.*

value – worth; consider something to be of worth.

   ✦ *We should value our parents.*

pets – animals that are tame and kept as companions.

   ✦ *Studies show that older people who have pets live longer than older people who live alone.*

PRACTICE

---

1. Fill in each of the blanks with the most appropriate vocabulary word.

   This _____ bird is found only on a small island in the Pacific.

   We had a _____ time at the birthday party.

Some people keep snakes and other reptiles as _____.

2. Can you make a list of five fruits?

_____   _____

_____   _____

_____

CONVERSATION

1. What is your favorite fruit? Have you ever picked fruit from a tree or bush? How old were you? Did you eat some?

2. Have you ever had a broken arm or a broken leg? How old were you? How did it happen?

3. Have you ever had a pet? What animal was your favorite pet? Did you take care of it? What animal would you like to have for a pet?

8

EAT HIS WORDS

USAGE

Jim predicted a Los Angeles Lakers victory in the NBA final playoffs, but he had to **eat his words** when the Dallas Mavericks won.

MEANING

A person is embarrassed when he has to **eat his words**. If someone has to **eat his words**, it means that what he said has proven to be false, and others know it. Perhaps he said his favorite team would win and then they lost. Perhaps he said that it wouldn't rain all weekend, and then it rained Saturday and Sunday. In either case, he had to **eat his words**.

STORY

Steve was an excellent car salesman. Every month the person who sold the most cars at the car lot received an extra $1,000 on his paycheck. Steve was ahead for the month of April. He teased the other salesmen. Steve said they did not have a chance. Then, on the final day of April, Fred sold three cars. Fred beat Steve, and Fred got the $1,000 bonus. Steve was embarrassed. He had to **eat his words**. He had to admit that Fred had beaten him. Fred laughed and the two men shook hands. They would compete again in May.

VOCABULARY

predicted – said something would happen in the future.

+ *The coach predicted the new player would be a star someday.*

embarrassed – feeling uncomfortable.

+ *The judge's questions about my personal life embarrassed me.*

bonus – an addition to what is usually given.

+ *The client gave his lawyer a bonus when he won the case.*

final – last in a series.

+ *The salesman said, "This is my final offer. Take it or leave it."*

compete – to take part in a contest.

+ *Thirty people were going to compete for the award.*

PRACTICE

1. Fill in the blank in each of the following sentences with the
   vocabulary word that best fits the meaning of the sentence.

   The baseball player received a _____ for each
   home run he hit.

   The announcer said, "This is the _____ call for
   Flight 294."

   Rene was training to _____ in the Boston
   Marathon.

2. Name five dishes you like to prepare for your friends.

   _____

   _____

   _____

   _____

   _____

CONVERSATION

1. Have you ever had to **eat your words**? What did you say?
   What happened? Can you laugh about it now?

2. What is your favorite sport? Which is your favorite team? Have you ever had to **eat your words** about a sports prediction?

Other choices: Another expression that means the same as **eat your words** is **swallow your words**. If you **swallow your words**, you have been shown to be wrong. Another related expression is **swallow your pride**. If you **swallow your pride**, you have to admit that someone else is right and you are wrong.

"In the course of my life, I have often had to eat my words, and I must confess that I have always found it a wholesome diet."

— *Winston Churchill (1874-1965),*
British Prime Minister and Statesman

SOMETHING IS FISHY

USAGE

I think **something is fishy** about the deal he is offering.

MEANING

If you think **something is fishy**, then you think something is suspicious. Perhaps someone seems untrustworthy. Perhaps you think someone is trying to cheat you. Perhaps you think someone is lying to you. Something is definitely wrong.

STORY

Aaron wanted to start his own business, but he did not have the necessary capital to get a good start. Because the economy was down, it was hard to get a loan from a bank. His friend told him about a man who would give him a loan. When Aaron read the contract the man had, it did not seem right. Aaron thought **something was fishy**. Aaron said, "I think I should have my lawyer look at this contract before I sign it. I want to feel good about what I'm signing. It's better to be safe rather than sorry."

VOCABULARY

suspicious – not trusting; not sure.

+ *Mario grew suspicious when Julio lied to him.*

economy – the general state of private and public business and money.

+ *The economy of Detroit depends on the success of its automobile industry.*

necessary – needed; basic.

+ *In the United States, it is necessary for children to get a smallpox vaccination before they attend school.*

capital – money used to make more money.

+ *Randy needed $50,000 more in capital to buy the restaurant.*

contract – a legal agreement.

+ *Ruth signed a contract promising to repay the loan in a year.*

PRACTICE

1. Fill in the blank in each of the following sentences with the most appropriate word from the vocabulary words.

   The football star signed a three year _____.

It seemed _____ to Alfonso that the car with two men sitting in it had been parked in front of his house for hours.

President Franklin D. Roosevelt created federal programs that improved the _____ during the 1930s in the United States.

2. Carefully read each of the following situations. If it seems fishy to you, circle *yes*. If it does not seem fishy to you, circle *no*.

A man on a street corner says he has a gold ring with a large diamond in it that he will sell you for $50.
Is this situation fishy? yes / no

Only 50,000 people were eligible to vote in the election, but there were 85,000 votes counted.
Is this situation fishy? yes / no

Bob and Ted tell their wives that they are going on a fishing trip for the weekend, but they do not take their fishing poles.
Is this situation fishy? yes / no

CONVERSATION

1. Have you ever been cheated by a salesperson? Have you ever been too trusting in a business deal? Are you more trusting or less trusting than you were when you were younger?

2. There is a saying, "If something seems too good to be true, it probably is." What does this mean? Do you agree?

Other choices: Another expression for **something is fishy** or **something smells fishy** is I **smell a rat.** When you know someone is lying to you or doing something wrong, you might say I **smell a rat.**

10

COUCH POTATO

USAGE

If you don't get moving, you'll become a **couch potato**.

MEANING

A **couch potato** is a person who watches television for hours and seems to stay in one place. If someone is a **couch potato**, he is glued to a spot and just sits. A couch potato is not being active. The expression **couch potato** suggests that the person is out of shape and sluggish. He is only interested in watching television.

STORY

Since Steve lost his job, he has become a **couch potato**. He just stays at home and watches television. His mother doesn't know what to do. She told him, "Turn off the TV and start looking for a job. Go out with your friends. Do something." He does not seem to hear what she is saying. He just sits there and watches TV. "It's like you're in a trance," his mother said. "You have become a **couch potato**."

VOCABULARY

---

couch – a piece of furniture that seats more than one person; a sofa.

+ *Three people can sit comfortably on the new couch in our living room.*

glued – stuck in one spot; pasted.

+ *The child glued sparkles on paper in art class.*

sluggish – without energy; moving slowly if at all.

+ *Until she had her coffee, Jane felt sluggish in the mornings.*

active – moving; interested; involved.

+ *Mila is a very active mother.*

trance – a state of not being aware; a state of not knowing what is happening in one's surroundings.

+ *The magician put Alex in a trance.*

PRACTICE

---

1. Choose the most appropriate, or apt, vocabulary words to fill in the blanks in the following sentences. Hint: the past tense of many verbs includes the letters "ed."

Jack _____ the newspaper article into his scrapbook.

The horse was _____ at the start, but he won the race.

Most Americans have a _____ in their living room.

2. Which of the following words fits you? Circle the words that you think accurately name or describe you.

cautious	modern	talkative	married
athletic	traditional	liberal	ambitious
healthy	playful	friendly	silly
smart	rich	kind	strong
short	calm	conservative	balanced
curious	happy	driven	busy
handsome	spiritual	retired	hardworking
serious	generous	polite	nice
lazy	comfortable	energetic	sad
tall	nervous	tired	confident
enthusiastic	shy	single	optimistic

How else can you describe yourself? What groups do you belong to? Sometimes we also describe ourselves as a member of a group.

I am a salesman. (driver/engineer/nanny/nurse)
I am a parent. (a sister, an uncle, an only child)

I am a _____.

I am also a _____.

CONVERSATION

1. If your son or daughter was acting like a **couch potato**, what would you do to change the situation?

2. How much television do you usually watch in a day? Do you watch more on Saturday? Is there a day you don't watch any television?

3. Have you ever felt it would be nice to just watch television all the time? Have you ever wished there were no television?

4. Which television shows are your favorites? Why?

5. If you had children, would you let them watch as much television as they wanted? Would you decide which programs they could watch? Why?

Other choices: Some other expressions that are similar to **couch potato** are **bump on a log,** which means not moving, and **stick in the mud,** which means not wanting to be active.

WALKING ON EGGSHELLS

USAGE

Since my father lost his job, I have been **walking on eggshells** whenever I am around him.

MEANING

One who is **walking on eggshells** is acting very carefully. One who is **walking on eggshells** is tense and worried about someone else's reaction. One who is **walking on eggshells** is trying to avoid unpleasantness.

STORY

Luis and Ernesto used to joke and tease with their father. He would laugh and tease them in return. Since their father lost his job, though, he has changed. He's no fun anymore. He gets angry when they try to play with him. He yells at them about every-thing. Luis and Ernesto have started **walking on eggshells** whenever they are around their father.

VOCABULARY

tense – uneasy; tight; anxious.

+ *Sam is always tense before midterm exams.*

reaction – a response to another person; a response to an idea or action.

+ *What was your reaction to the President's speech about the nuclear treaty?*

avoid – stay away from; stay clear of.

+ *Sheila avoids her former boyfriend.*

unpleasantness – not being pleasant; not being enjoyable.

+ *I lose my appetite when there is unpleasantness at mealtime.*

tease – make fun of in a joking way.

+ *Bob likes to tease Barbara about her red hair.*

PRACTICE

1. Fill each blank in the following sentences with the appropriate vocabulary word.

   I always feel less _____ after a massage.

   My aunt Nancy tries very hard to avoid _____.

Uncle Joe would tell jokes and _____ the girls whenever he came for a visit.

2. Use the phrase **walking on eggshells** as an idiom in a sentence. Your sentence should show that you know the meaning of the expression **walking on eggshells**.

_____

_____

CONVERSATION

1. If one actually tried to **walk on eggshells**, what would happen?

2. In your experience, why do people **walk on eggshells**?

3. Have you ever been in a situation in which you felt like you were **walking on eggshells**? What were you afraid was going to happen?

Other choices: Instead of saying **walking on eggshells**, you might say **treating with kid gloves**, which means being extra careful with someone who gets easily upset. Kid gloves are gloves made from very soft leather.

> "I know that when I was a full-blown, practicing alcoholic, everyone used to walk around me on eggshells."
>
> — *Eric Clapton (1945-), singer and songwriter*

PIE IN THE SKY

USAGE

His goal of being an NBA basketball star was **pie in the sky**.

MEANING

If an idea is **pie in the sky**, it is unrealistic. It is a fantasy. If a girl who can't act believes she will one day win an Oscar for best actress, it is **pie in the sky**. If a boy who can't play basketball thinks he will someday play in the NBA, it is **pie in the sky**.

STORY

Matt was in his final year of high school. His grades were below average. Matt had never done his school assignments. He had never studied for his examinations. His mother worked hard as a cleaning lady and supported him and her three younger children. When Matt's school counselor asked him what he was going to do after he graduated, Matt said, "I am going to get a scholarship and go to college."

The counselor said, "Matt, who will give you such a scholarship? You have bad grades. You have never shown that you can do the work. You need a realistic, practical plan. This plan is **pie in the sky**."

VOCABULARY

goal – an aim; a plan for the future.

✦ *goal is a combination of realistic thinking and hope.*

unrealistic – not realistic; probably not possible; not based on reality.

✦ *Without a job and savings, it is unrealistic for Jake to think that the bank will give him a loan for a house.*

average – the usual kind or amount.

✦ *Paulo was happy that his grades were above average.*

assignments – a lesson or task that a teacher or boss expects.

✦ *Mother said I could watch TV after I finished my homework assignments.*

counselor – a person whose job is to give advice.

✦ *The school counselor helped Leslie apply for a scholarship.*

PRACTICE

1. Fill in the blank in each of the following sentences with the vocabulary word that best fits the meaning of the sentence.

   The students smiled when the teacher said, "There are no homework _____ for this weekend."

   The school _____ talked with Sue about her grades.

   It is _____ to expect that Juan's novel will become a bestseller.

2. Can you name five kinds of pie?

   _____   _____

   _____   _____

   _____

CONVERSATION

1. What is your favorite type of pie? Do you bake it? Do you buy it? Does someone else in your family bake it for you?

2. Have you ever had a dream that others said was unrealistic? Did you take practical steps to make your dream come true? Were you successful? Are you working toward a dream now?

3. Sometimes unlikely things do happen. For his first two years in high school, Michael Jordan did not make his school's basketball team. Yet he went on to become an NBA superstar. Do you know other stories about unlikely dreams becoming true?

> "You'll get pie in the sky when you die."
> *Joe Hill (1879-1915),*
> *American songwriter and union organizer*

MORE FOOD PHRASES

Apple of His Eye

USAGE

Fiona, his daughter, is the **apple of his eye.**

MEANING

If she is **the apple of his eye,** he centers his life on her. He loves her dearly.

_____

The Big Cheese

USAGE

Paul thinks he is **the big cheese.**

MEANING

If he thinks he is **the big cheese,** he thinks he is the most important person. He thinks he is the best. He sees himself as the star.

_____

A Bad Egg

USAGE

I think Mike is **a bad egg.**

MEANING

A bad egg is one who cannot be trusted. **A bad egg** is one who gets into trouble.

The Cream of the Crop

USAGE

This race horse is **the cream of the crop**.

MEANING

If something is **the cream of the crop**, it is the best. Just like cream rises to the top of milk, it is the top of the top.

Sell like Hot Cakes

USAGE

Take it from me. This dress will **sell like hot cakes**.

MEANING

If something **sells like hot cakes**, it will be very popular. It will be bought by many people.

Take it with a Grain of Salt

USAGE

She predicts this stock will rise 50% within the year. I think you should **take that with a grain of salt**.

MEANING

If you take a statement **with a grain of salt**, you do not completely trust it. You doubt that it is true.

In a Nutshell

USAGE

In a nutshell, I think you should try and refinance your home rather than walk away from it and ruin your credit.

MEANING

In a nutshell means to say the most important part as simply as possible.

_____

The Bread Winner

USAGE

In a traditional family, the father is usually the main **bread winner**.

MEANING

The **bread winner** is the person who provides the money for the daily needs of the family, like food and housing.

_____

Spice Up

USAGE

Wear a red scarf to **spice up** your outfit.

MEANING

Spice up means to make it more exciting.

Soup Up

USAGE

John **souped up** his car with fancy gold hubcaps.

MEANING

To **soup up** means to make it faster or fancier. Soup up usually applies to cars and trucks.

FOOD FOR THOUGHT:
REVIEW OF UNIT TWO

Match the sentence on the left with the appropriate idiom on the right. See example #1.

Example: Susan was careful to not make any trouble.
Answer: E. She was **walking on eggshells**.

————————

_____ 1. Susan was careful to not make any trouble.

A. This is **a piece of cake**.

_____ 2. Sam was in trouble.

B. You are a **couch potato**.

_____ 3. That plan has no chance.

C. He was **in a pickle**.

_____ 4. You watch too much TV.

D. That is **pie in the sky**.

_____ 5. This is so easy.

E. She was **walking on eggshells**.

_____ 6. Grace had to apologize for what she had said.

F. She had to **eat her words**.

UNIT THREE
BODY LANGUAGE

We live in our bodies. Each body part has a name. Sometimes we also use these body part names to express other ideas. At times the connection is clear. We may refer to **the leg of a chair** or **the head of a school**. If we know the meaning of the words leg and head, we can probably guess the meaning for **leg of a chair** or **the head of a school**.

The farm intern is learning about farming. He's wet behind the ears.

Sometimes, though, the meaning is not so clear. What does it mean if you say someone is **thin skinned**? Or what does it mean if a person says, "He's **wet behind the ears**"? The lessons in this unit consider common American expressions in which body parts are used in uncommon ways.

A PAIN IN THE NECK

USAGE

My new neighbor plays loud music all the time; he is **a pain in the neck**.

MEANING

If someone is **a pain in the neck**, he is annoying. He is a pest. Perhaps he is a neighbor who is always asking for help. Perhaps he is someone at work who is always complaining. Perhaps he is a boss who is too strict. Someone who is **a pain in the neck** is as irritating as a real pain in your neck would be.

STORY

Celeste's sister-in-law called her each day. She would ask about Celeste's plans, or she would ask what Celeste was cooking for dinner. She would ask what Celeste was wearing. Often she would find fault with Celeste. She tried to boss her around and tell her what to do. Celeste's sister-in-law was **a pain in the neck**. Celeste did not argue with her, though, because she did not want to cause any trouble in the family.

VOCABULARY

---

neighbor – a person who lives nearby, often next door.

+ *My neighbor and I often help each other.*

annoy – to cause bad feelings; to create unhappiness.

+ *Getting stuck in traffic annoys me – especially when I'm running late.*

pest – a person who is a bother; a person who is annoying.

+ *Sophia's little brother is often a pest when she is trying to talk on the phone.*

strict – enforcing the rules; demanding that all details be correct.

+ *We have strict rules about being late for our college class.*

sister-in-law – the person who married one's brother.

+ *Tanya's sister-in-law shared her special recipe for stuffed cabbage with Tanya.*

PRACTICE

---

1. Fill in the blank in each of the following sentences with the vocabulary word that best fits the meaning of the sentence.

   Juan and his _____ play football each Saturday.

Chris' father was very _____ with him.

The mole in my garden is a _____.

2. Your in-laws are the people to whom you are related by marriage. Correctly fill in the blanks in the following sentences.

Example: The mother of your wife is your mother-in-law.

The father of your wife is your _____.

The brother of your wife is your _____.

The sister of your wife is your _____.

Your son's wife is your _____.

Your daughter's husband is your _____.

CONVERSATION

1. Do you know someone who is **a pain in the neck**? What does this person do? How do you respond?

2. In the story, Celeste does not argue with her sister-in-law. What else could she do? What do you think she should do? How would you handle this situation?

3. What are some things that a boss who is a **pain in the neck** might do at work?

14

PULLING YOUR LEG

USAGE

That cannot be true. Are you **pulling my leg**?

MEANING

If a person is **pulling your leg**, he is teasing you. The person may be saying something that is not true. The person may be exaggerating about something he saw or did. He may be trying to fool you. If you say, "you are **pulling my leg**," it means you understand what is happening. You get the joke. Usually, both of you will then laugh together. If someone is **pulling your leg**, it is all just for fun.

STORY

Rafi and Jimmie were good friends. They enjoyed playing tricks on each other. One day Rafi called Jimmie on his phone. Rafi tried to sound as if he were someone else. He tried to sound serious and adult. He said to Jimmie, "Congratulations Mr. Smith, you have won the lottery. You have won four million dollars."

For a second, Jimmie was fooled. Then he said, "What? Rafi, is that you? Are you **pulling my leg**?" Then they laughed together.

VOCABULARY

exaggerating – making something more than it is, such as bigger or funnier.

✦ *David was exaggerating when he said he caught an eighty pound trout fish on his fishing trip.*

tricks – an act to fool people.

✦ *The children were delighted with the clown's magic tricks.*

serious – not joking; important.

✦ *Was the car accident serious? Did anyone get hurt?*

adult – fully grown; mature.

✦ *You must be an adult to truly understand this movie.*

lottery – a game of chance used by governments to raise money.

✦ *How would you spend the money if you won the lottery?*

PRACTICE

1. Fill in each of the blanks in the following sentences with the appropriate vocabulary word from your list.

   You must buy a _____ ticket in order to win.

   My older brother Roy can do _____ on his bicycle.

   The judge said, "This is a very _____ charge."

2. Make a list of five parts of the human body.

   _____   _____

   _____   _____

   _____

CONVERSATION

1. Do you like to tease other people? What is the most enjoyable trick you ever played on someone else? What is the most enjoyable trick someone else played on you?

2. If a person catches an eight-pound fish and tells other people he caught an eighty-pound fish, he is exaggerating. If a person is on a diet and loses six pounds but tells other people he lost eleven pounds, he is exaggerating. Why do people sometimes exaggerate? Can you think of other examples of exaggeration? Have you ever exaggerated?

TURNS A BLIND EYE

USAGE

My mother usually **turns a blind eye** when my brothers fight.

MEANING

If someone **turns a blind eye**, the person acts like he does not see or care about what is happening. If someone **turns a blind eye**, the person pretends to not know what is going on. A politician might **turn a blind eye** to bribery and corruption. A worker might **turn a blind eye** to his manager's cheating. A wife might turn a blind eye to her husband's faults. If you **turn a blind eye**, you have decided to **see no evil** and act as if you know nothing.

STORY

Stacy had worked at the jewelry store for three years. She knew the real worth of each diamond ring in the store. Stacy overheard the manager of the store tell a customer that one of the rings was worth much more than it really was. The customer did not know anything about diamonds. What could Stacy do? If she said anything to the customer, she might get fired. She did not want the customer to be cheated, but she did not want to be fired. Stacy decided she had to **turn a blind eye** to the manager's misleading words.

VOCABULARY

blind - not able to see.

+ *The blind man crossed the street with the help of a seeing-eye dog and a cane.*

pretends - to act as if something is real or true when it is not.

+ *Pierre pretends that his business is doing better than it really is.*

bribe - money given so someone breaks the rule; an illegal gift to an official.

+ *Bribes can cause many problems and hurt many innocent people.*

corruption - wrongdoing; illegal or immoral acts.

+ *Corruption is when police officers take bribes to break rules.*

diamond - a precious gem, usually colorless.

+ *Jim gave Yuni a lovely diamond engagement ring.*

PRACTICE

1. Use words from your vocabulary list to correctly fill in the blanks in the following sentences.

   A _____ is one of the most popular gems.

   The artist Paul Gauguin became _____ when he was older.

   A bad, corrupt policeman takes _____, lets criminals escape, and **turns a blind eye.**

2. Read about each of the following situations. If you think the person who is described is **turning a blind eye**, circle *Yes*. If you think the person being described is not **turning a blind eye** in that situation, circle *No*.

   Pierre saw a man put a package of meat in his coat pocket at the grocery store. The man walked out without paying. Pierre did not tell anyone what he saw. Did Pierre **turn a blind eye?**

   Yes / No

   Carol and Suzanne sat next to each other in class. Carol saw Suzanne cheat on the final exam. Carol did not tell the teacher. Did Carol **turn a blind eye?**

   Yes / No

Alice saw a speeding car run into a parked car, seriously dent it, and leave without stopping. Alice copied down the license plate number of the speeding car and left it with a note on the windshield of the dented car. Did Alice **turn a blind eye**?

Yes / No

When Isaac looked out his apartment window, he saw three men from his apartment building beat up an older man. They also took the man's wallet. When the police asked Isaac if he had seen anything, he said no. Did Isaac **turn a blind eye**?

Yes / No

CONVERSATION

1. In what kinds of situations do you **turn a blind eye**?

2. When might people have gotten in trouble because they **turned a blind eye**? Why?

3. Why not **turn a blind eye**?

WET BEHIND THE EARS

USAGE

Do not expect too much; he is still **wet behind the ears**.

MEANING

Someone who is **wet behind the ears** is young and inexperienced.

STORY

David was a sixteen-year-old boy who had always lived in the suburbs of Chicago. He knew he needed to get a job during his summer vacation to save some money for college. He also knew he wanted to get different experiences. David's Uncle Ned was a farmer who hired extra farm hands during the summer to help with the chores. Uncle Ned agreed to hire David for minimum wage to work on his farm. David did not know how to milk a cow. He did not know how to drive a tractor. He did not even know how to ride a horse. When the other farm hands laughed at him, Uncle Ned said, "Give him time. He's still **wet behind the ears**. He'll learn."

VOCABULARY

inexperienced – without practice; without skill or experience.

+ *The young man was eager but inexperienced.*

suburbs – an area of homes bordering a city.

+ *The suburbs around Chicago grew rapidly after World War II.*

chores – physical jobs on a farm or ranch, such as milking, plowing, etc.

+ *Feeding the horses was one of David's daily chores.*

minimum – the least amount allowed.

+ *It is hard to support a family if you earn only minimum wage.*

wages – money earned for work done; payment.

+ *Steve always gave 10% of his wages to his church.*

PRACTICE

1. Study the vocabulary words. Then fill in each of the blanks in the following sentences with the most apt vocabulary word.

   The state deducts taxes from my _____.

When she moved to the _____, Alice was able to have a garden with vegetables and many beautiful flowers.

"The _____ passing grade is 60%," the teacher said.

2. Use the idiom **wet behind the ears** in a sentence.

_____

_____

CONVERSATION

1. What are some of the jobs that a farm hand needs to do? Have you ever done any of these jobs? If you worked on a farm, what chores would you like to do? What chores would you not want to do?

2. Can you think of other expressions in English that mention parts of the human body? Can you guess what it means to be **strong hearted**? Can you guess what it means if something **costs an arm and a leg**? Can you guess what it means to say you cannot **stomach** a person or thing?

Other choices: To say someone is **green** at his job is the same as to say he is **wet behind the ears**. Both **green** and **wet behind the ears** mean new to the job and inexperienced.

17

THIN SKINNED

USAGE

He is difficult to work with because he is so **thin skinned.**

MEANING

If a person is **thin skinned**, it means his feelings are easily hurt. He gets upset at the slightest correction or rejection. He might even imagine a criticism or rejection when none is meant. If others do not wish to upset him, they have to be very careful around him because he is so **thin skinned.**

STORY

Steve was a lawyer at a big company. The secretary he had for twenty years retired, and he hired Helen as the new secretary. Helen was young, had excellent grades, and seemed very qualified for the job. After a few weeks, though, Steve realized that Helen was difficult for him to work with. She was too **thin skinned.** Every time Steve tried to explain something to her, Helen got upset.

Steve told another lawyer, "I cannot relax around Helen. She gets upset so easily. Whenever I want to show her how I want something done, she acts as if I'm saying she is dumb. She is too **thin skinned**. How can we possibly work with her?"

VOCABULARY

correction – a change to make something better or more accurate.

   ✦ *Ned made a slight correction to the lens setting on his camera.*

rejection – being turned down or not being accepted.

   ✦ *A writer may get many rejections before he is published.*

retired – finished with work or career because of age.

   ✦ *After thirty winning seasons, Coach Riley retired.*

lawyer – a person who has qualified to practice law; an attorney.

   ✦ *A good lawyer always protects his client's interests.*

relax – be at ease; be comfortable.

   ✦ *On Sundays I usually relax with my family.*

PRACTICE

1. Fill in the blanks in the following sentences with the most apt words from your vocabulary list.

   A _____ should always be respectful toward the jury.

   These shoes will help make a _____ in your posture.

   When Anna _____, she traveled to many different countries.

2. Read each of the following sentences. If you think the sentence describes someone who is **thin skinned,** circle *Yes*. If the sentence describes someone who is not **thin skinned**, circle *No.*

   When Amy did not get a role in the play, she started crying.
   Yes / No

   Mrs. Adams was a tough teacher, but I learned a lot from her.
   Yes / No

   The two boys traded insults with each other and laughed.
   Yes / No

   John said, "Criticism only makes me stronger."
   Yes / No

   The boy quit the soccer team after the coach yelled at him.
   Yes / No

CONVERSATION

1. Since **thin skinned** means someone who is easily upset by correction or rejection, what do you think **thick skinned** means?

2. When might it be helpful to be **thick skinned**? Can you think of jobs that might require you to be **thick skinned** in order to be successful?

3. If a person is learning to play guitar, he may soak his fingertips in vinegar to toughen the skin on the end of his fingers. Soft fingertips may get cut and bleed easily when he is learning to play the guitar. With tough fingertips, a person can practice without getting cut. With tough fingertips, a person can learn to play beautiful music. If someone is emotionally **thin skinned**, what can he do to toughen himself? What suggestions do you have for someone who is **thin skinned**?

Other choices: See **walk on eggshells**. If one does not want to upset a person who is **thin skinned,** one may have to **walk on eggshells** around him.

OUT OF YOUR MIND

USAGE

If you think I'm going to wear that swimsuit, you're **out of your mind.**

MEANING

The expression **out of your mind** means the suggestion is not realistic; the suggestion is crazy; the suggestion is ridiculous; the suggestion is outrageous; the suggestion is unthinkable.

STORY

Jock was bored. He felt like doing something he hadn't done for a while. He called his friend Ian and asked him if he'd like to go to the movies. "We'll find something good," said Jock. "We'll drive by the theater and see what's playing."

"Okay," said Ian. "See you soon." When they got to the mall, the sign in the ticket window said that ticket prices had risen. The price was now $15 for each ticket. Ian said to Jock, "If you think I'm paying $15 for a movie ticket, you're **out of your mind. That's ridiculous."**

VOCABULARY

outrageous – describing a situation which is very wrong; a situation that makes one angry.

✦ *It is outrageous that before child labor laws, six-year-old children used to work in the mines.*

bored – having no interest; feeling dull; feeling blah.

✦ *People who are easily bored are often boring to others.*

mall – a collection of stores, restaurants, and theaters in the same area, often under one roof.

✦ *Robert shops at the mall because it is nearby and convenient.*

price – the cost; the amount of money to purchase an item.

✦ *A sale price is cheaper than the regular price.*

ridiculous – a subject for ridicule; a subject for laughter or sarcasm.

✦ *My sister's five-inch high-heeled shoes seem ridiculous to me.*

PRACTICE

1. Fill in the blanks in the following sentences with the appropriate words from the vocabulary list.

There are three Chinese restaurants at that

_____.

If farm fields get too much rain, the _____ of
fruits and vegetables goes up for customers in grocery stores.

If a person enjoys reading, he is seldom _____.

2. List three things or experiences whose price you think is too
   high.

   _____

   _____

   _____

CONVERSATION

1. If a person's hat is ridiculous, we might smile at it. If a
   person is treated unfairly, we might become angry. What
   things or experiences in American culture today seem
   ridiculous or outrageous to you? What responses do you have
   to these situations?

2. When you feel bored, what do you do to change your mood?
   Does taking a walk help change your feeling? Does cooking a
   good meal help? Does phoning a friend help change your
   feeling? Does watching a television show make you feel
   better? Do you have other suggestions for boredom?

MORE BODY LANGUAGE

There are many more examples of body parts used in common expressions. Here are more that are easy to understand and use.

Play it by Ear

USAGE

Stephen likes to **play it by ear**.

MEANING

Stephen doesn't like to make plans, but prefers to see how things unfold naturally.

A Leg to Stand on

USAGE

You don't have **a leg to stand on**.

MEANING

There is no support for what you are claiming.

Broad Shoulders

USAGE

I have got **broad shoulders**.

MEANING

I am strong enough to handle troubles and/or criticism.

An Arm and a Leg

USAGE

My new car cost **an arm and a leg.**

MEANING

My new car was very expensive.

_____

Eyes on the Prize

USAGE

Kristin keeps her **eyes on the prize.**

MEANING

Kristin stays focused on achieving her goal.

_____

Elbow Room

USAGE

Give me some **elbow room.**

MEANING

You are too close for my comfort.

Put Your Foot in Your Mouth

USAGE

Franco **put his foot in his mouth** when he met Jane's parents.

MEANING

Franco said something he should not have said.

————————

Have Your Finger in a Lot of Pies

USAGE

John has his **finger in a lot of pies.**

MEANING

John seems to have many business deals, but I am not sure what he really does.

————————

Stick Your Nose in

USAGE

Greta **sticks her nose in** other people's business.

MEANING

Greta is pushy and wants to know too much personal information about other people.

The Cold Shoulder

USAGE

Why is Lee giving me **the cold shoulder**?

MEANING

Lee is ignoring me.

Turn a Deaf Ear

USAGE

Sam turns a deaf ear to my pleas.

MEANING

Sam pretended that he didn't hear what I said. He ignored me.

BODY BUILDING:
REVIEW OF UNIT THREE

Match the correct expression with the meaning of the sentence. You may look at the lessons to find your answers. See #1 as an example.

Example: 1. Jim teasingly said I won the lottery.
Answer: E. He was **pulling my leg.**

––––––––––

____ 1. Jim teasingly said I won the lottery.

A. She is **thin-skinned.**

____ 2. This dress was very expensive.

B. He is **wet behind the ears.**

____ 3. Brian is a new recruit.

C. He **turned a deaf ear.**

____ 4. Joan gets upset about everything.

D. She is **a pain in the neck.**

____ 5. Sally did not even say hello to me.

E. He was **pulling my leg.**

_____ 6. I begged Bob for help, but he pretended he did not hear me.

F. She **sticks her nose** in my business.

_____ 7. My sister is a pest.

G. It **cost an arm and a leg.**

_____ 8. Laura wants to know everything about my personal life.

H. She gave me **the cold shoulder**.

_____ 9. The boss heard Mary insult his wife.

I. He heard her **put her foot** in her mouth.

UNIT FOUR

ANIMAL WISDOM

We live with animals in our world. Many of us have pets. We know about dogs and cats. We know what cows, pigs, and chickens look like. Even if we have never seen them, we know lions, elephants, deer, and camels.

Many idioms have come from our special relationships with animals.

We teach young children the names of animals at the same time we teach them numbers and colors. Information about animals is part of the basic information we share as human beings. Thus, it is under-standable that we often use animals in our daily language when we are trying to describe our feelings and ideas.

What does it mean if a friend tells you, "I **let the cat out of the bag**"? What does it mean when someone complains, "That teacher **gets my goat**"?

The following lessons will help you understand some common American expressions that use animals to help describe people and our world.

LET THE CAT OUT OF THE BAG

USAGE

Please, whatever you do, don't **let the cat out of the bag!**

MEANING

The expression don't **let the cat out of the bag** means to not repeat this secret to others.

STORY

Kathy was planning a surprise birthday party for Jack's 30th birthday. She told their friends, "Keep this quiet. I want this to be a surprise. Don't **let the cat out of the bag!**"

The day of the party, Jack's boss Eddie told Jack he was sorry that he wouldn't be able to come to the birthday party. Then Eddie said, "Oh no, I **let the cat out of the bag.**"

VOCABULARY

---

bag – a sack made of cloth, paper, or plastic.

- ✦ *The grocery clerk asked, "Do you want a paper bag or a plastic bag?"*

secret – information which is hidden from others.

- ✦ **Laura kept her diary in a secret drawer in her desk.*

birthday – the anniversary of one's birth.

- ✦ *Roy's birthday was September 1st.*

boss – supervisor; the person in charge of others.

- ✦ *Steve's boss expects him to work overtime every Friday.*

surprise – something unexpected.

- ✦ *It was a surprise when the shortest competitor won the high jump.*

PRACTICE

---

1. Choose the vocabulary word that best fills in the blank in each of the following sentences.

   I want theater tickets for my _____.

   Santa Claus is shown with a _____ full of toys on his back.

The _____ said that December had been a good month for sales.

2. The cat family includes many different types of cats, tame and wild. List five types of cats you know.

_____   _____

_____   _____

_____

CONVERSATION

1. Have you ever **let the cat out of the bag**? What happened? Were others angry with you?

2. Benjamin Franklin wrote, "Three can keep a secret if two of them are dead." What does this mean? Do you agree?

Other choices: Other expressions similar to **let the cat out of the bag** are **spill the beans** or **give away**. If you **spill the beans** or **give something away**, you have told information that you were not supposed to tell.

> "Lettin' the cat outta the bag is a whole lot easier 'n than puttin' it back in."
>
> — *Will Rogers (1879-1935),*
> *American cowboy, actor, and comedian*

20

GETS MY GOAT

USAGE

When I hear my boss lie to his wife on the phone, it **gets my goat**.

MEANING

If something **gets my goat**, it irritates me.
If something **gets my goat**, it angers me.

STORY

John owned a grocery store in a small town. He knew everyone in town, and everyone in town knew him. He was always friendly with his customers. He made free home deliveries for his older customers. He always stayed pleasant, even with people who were difficult. One morning when John came to open his store, he found the front window had been smashed with a brick. Inside, the store was a big mess. Shelves had been pushed over. Cartons of milk had been spilled on the floor, and eggs had been thrown at the walls. "This is terrible," he told the police. "It makes no sense. Why would anyone do this to me? It really **gets my goat.**"

VOCABULARY

goat – a farm animal that is used to produce milk and cheese.

+ *Goats are sure-footed, even on rocks and mountains.*

customer – a person buying a product or service.

+ *A good salesman is always polite to his customers.*

town – a place where people live that is larger than a village and smaller than a city.

+ *Even though it was a small town, my hometown had a public library, a fire station, and a police station.*

deliveries – taking merchandise from one location to another.

+ *The United States Post Office never makes deliveries on Sundays.*

shelves – horizontal supports that hold items like books and dishes.

+ *We made sturdy book shelves from bricks and wood.*

PRACTICE

1. Fill in each of the blanks in the following sentences with the most apt vocabulary word.

   Li is allergic to cow cheese, but he can eat _____ cheese.

There is an American saying that "The _____ is always right."

Stan drove through rain and snow to make pizza _____.

2. List three advantages to living in a small town rather than in a big city.

_____

_____

_____

3. List three advantages to living in a big city rather than in a small town.

_____

_____

_____

CONVERSATION

1. Would you rather live in a town or a city? What are the main reasons for your choice? Do you think life is easier in a town or in a city?

2. Is there someone or something that **gets your goat**? Who or what is it? How do you act? What do you say?

21

THE ELEPHANT IN THE ROOM

USAGE

It seems to me that **the elephant in the room** is Stan's broken engagement.

MEANING

The elephant in the room is a circumstance that everyone is aware of, but no one wants to talk about. Probably no one is talking about **the elephant in the room** because the subject is embarrassing. If there is an **elephant in the room**, people are uncomfortable and feel they can not discuss something in an honest way.

STORY

Nancy had invited ten friends to dinner. When she described what was on her menu, everyone was excited. It sounded delicious. When they arrived, though, there was a burned smell in the air. And when they ate the meat, it was clear to everyone that it had been overcooked. It was dry and stringy. No one said anything about the meat, though. No one wanted to hurt Nancy's feelings. It was like an **elephant in the room.**

VOCABULARY

---

elephant – a large animal with a thick skin, a long trunk, and two tusks.

✦ *The elephant is the largest of the four-legged animals.*

embarrassing – something that makes one feel uncomfortable; attention that is unwanted.

✦ *It was embarrassing when the best man at the wedding lost the ring for the wedding ceremony.*

burned – ruined by fire or heat; charred.

✦ *Mary burned the letter in the fireplace.*

delicious – pleasant to smell; pleasant to taste.

✦ *The chocolate cake was delicious.*

stringy – like string; in strands.

✦ *Stringy meat is hard to chew.*

PRACTICE

---

1. Use your vocabulary words to correctly fill in the blanks in the following sentences. Hint: Watch the verb tense and remember to use "ed" for regular verbs.

   It was _____ when Ann forgot her lines during the play.

Did you see an _____ at the zoo?

I lost the wedding picture of my parents when the house

_____.

2. An adjective is a word that describes a noun. For example, in the phrase *pretty* girl, *pretty* is the adjective. List five adjectives that might describe an elephant.

_____   _____

_____   _____

_____

CONVERSATION

1. Have you ever seen an elephant up close? Where? What did you think about the elephant you saw?

2. Have you ever been in a situation in which everyone knew what was wrong, but no one mentioned it?

22

DARK HORSE

USAGE

Seabiscuit was a great American racehorse. He started out as a **dark horse**, but went on to win major races and the hearts of the American people.

MEANING

The **dark horse** is a competitor who is not favored to win, but he does have a chance to win. If the **dark horse** wins, it is an upset victory. A **dark horse** might be a candidate who is not expected to win in a political election. A **dark horse** might be an athlete who is not expected to win. A **dark horse** might be a movie that is competing for an award. In each case, the **dark horse** is not expected to win – but it might win.

STORY

Many movie plots are about a **dark horse** who beats the favorite. In the movie *Rocky*, Sylvester Stallone plays a **dark horse** prize fighter who beats the champion. In the movie *Hoosiers*, an unknown small town high school basketball team, definitely a **dark horse**, defeats many teams from larger schools and wins the State Championship. When a **dark horse** wins, it is very dramatic.

VOCABULARY

upset victory – an unexpected win; a win against the odds.

> ✦ *When Seabiscuit beat War Admiral, it was an upset victory.*

candidate – a person competing for a political office; a person being considered for a job.

> ✦ *Political candidates give many speeches.*

competitor – one who competes; one who works toward victory.

> ✦ *Jesse Owens was a strong competitor in the '36 Olympics.*

plot – the story line; the summary of action.

> ✦ *The teacher asked us to summarize the plot of Hamlet.*

champion – the top competitor; the one who beats all others.

> ✦ *Muhammad Ali was a champion heavyweight boxer.*

PRACTICE

1. Fill in the blanks in the following sentences with the vocabulary words that best complete the sentences.

A gold medal in an Olympic event goes to the

_____.

There were many twists and surprises in the book's

_____.

The _____ for the School Board was a retired teacher.

2. A common American term that is similar to **dark horse** is **underdog**. If two dogs are fighting, the dog that is on top would be expected to win. The underdog would not be expected to win. Do you prefer the term **dark horse** or do you prefer the term **underdog**?

Use the term **dark horse** in a sentence about politics.

_____

_____

Use the term **underdog** in a sentence about sports.

_____

_____

CONVERSATION

1. Have you ever been the **dark horse** and surprised people when you won? What happened? How did you feel?

2. Have you ever cheered for the **dark horse** in a political election or a sporting event in which the **dark horse** won? What happened? How did you feel?

3. Have you ever cheered for a **dark horse** in a political election or sporting event in which the **dark horse** lost? What happened? How did you feel?

4. Since people want to be winners, why would anyone ever support the **dark horse**?

5. What are the possible pitfalls of being the one who is expected to win?

LIKE A FISH OUT OF WATER

USAGE

Bob was the only male in the class, and he felt **like a fish out of water**.

MEANING

If a person feels **like a fish out of water**, he is in a situation that makes him feel out of place and awkward. When a fish is out of water, it flops back and forth. Sometimes a person, too, feels upset when he or she is not in a familiar setting. The person feels **like a fish out of water**.

STORY

When Ken took Susie to meet his parents in their home, she felt uncomfortable. Their estate was huge, and they had servants. Such riches felt strange to her. She felt awkward and uneasy. She said to Ken, "I feel **like a fish out of water**."

He said, "They will love you, honey. Don't worry."

VOCABULARY

uncomfortable - not at ease; feeling discomfort.

+ *Anne felt uncomfortable in large crowds.*

flop – turn back and forth; fall down clumsily.

+ *Toddlers often flop on the floor.*

situation – circumstance; incident; surroundings.

+ *The situation is tense in the final minutes of a close basketball game.*

familiar – known; usual; comfortable.

+ *Anne thought the newcomer looked familiar, but she couldn't remember his name.*

huge – very large.

+ *It was a huge mistake for Juan to party all night before the final exam.*

PRACTICE

1. Fill in each blank in the following sentences with the most appropriate vocabulary word.

The lawyer said to the jury, "Once you know the

_____, I'm sure you will find my client not guilty."

When I remember the silly things I did when I was younger, I feel rather _____.

My brother ate a _____ piece of cherry pie for dessert.

2. Describe a situation in which a person feels **like a fish out of water**. Use the idiom **like a fish out of water** in your example.

_____

_____

CONVERSATION

1. Have you ever felt **like a fish out of water**? Did you later feel at ease in that situation? What changed?

2. Do you have any suggestions to help people feel more at ease when they are nervous? Does taking a deep breath help you? Does counting sheep help you? Does picturing other people wearing pajamas help you?

3. Have you ever visited an aquarium or Sea World? What kind of fish did you see? Did you have a favorite?

Other choices: Another expression that means a person is out of place in his surroundings is **like a bull in a china shop**. Can you imagine a bull in a china shop? He would have no idea how to act. He would break many beautiful things.

> "That song is just about feeling like a fish out of water."
> *Jon Crosby (1976-), American musician*

(24)

LET'S TALK TURKEY

USAGE

The President said to Congress, **"Let's talk turkey."**

MEANING

Let's talk turkey means let's talk realistically; let's talk seriously; let's talk truthfully; let's be real with each other and get down to business.

STORY

Rose knew she needed another car, but she also knew she couldn't afford a new car. She wondered if she should buy a used car or if she should lease a new car. Since she didn't know what to look for, she asked her uncle, who was an automobile mechanic, to advise her. "We'll find you a good used car," he said. "I'll go with you." When they got to the used car lot, a salesman immediately greeted them. As they wandered around the lot looking at the cars, he gave them a sales pitch on each car. Finally, Rose's uncle said, "We might be interested in this one, but the price is too high for this model and year. Also, we need to know what kind of guarantee you offer."

The salesman said, "Step into my office, and **let's talk turkey**. I think we can make a deal."

VOCABULARY

lease – to rent for a stated time; the contract by which one rents.

✦ *Juan signed an apartment lease for one year.*

mechanic – a qualified person who works on a machine.

✦ *The mechanic said that Ed's car needed a new transmission.*

advise – to speak with authority and give advice.

✦ *Ivan's career counselor advised him to improve his English skills.*

wandered – went from place to place without a clear pattern.

✦ *The child in the store wandered from one toy to another.*

sales pitch – information a salesman gives a customer when he is trying to sell a product.

✦ *Top salesmen always have a good sales pitch.*

PRACTICE

1. Fill in each of the blanks in the following sentences with the appropriate word from the vocabulary list.

The lawyer said, "I _____ you to sign a plea agreement."

Some people _____ furniture for big parties in their home.

The insurance salesman was pleasant, but I did not believe his _____.

2. List three situations in which the idiom **let's talk turkey** might be used.

_____

_____

_____

CONVERSATION

1. Rose knew she needed a car, but she didn't know anything about car engines. People often have to make decisions about purchases that they do not know much about. What suggestions do you have for checking about a purchase before you buy it?

2. Have you ever been persuaded by a sales pitch and then discovered you bought something that does not work as the sales person said it would? What did you do? What can someone do in that situation?

MORE ON ANIMAL WISDOM

Since we share a knowledge of animals, we often use this animal information to describe people. Read aloud the following common expressions. What do they mean? Can you add to this list?

She is as soft as a kitten.

She is as sweet as a kitten.

He is as strong as an ox.

He is as strong as a bull.

She is as mad as a wet hen.

He is as sly as a fox.

He is as tricky as a coyote.

She is as messy as a pig.

He eats like a pig.

She is as fat as a pig.

She is as timid as a mouse.

He is as wise as an owl.

He can swim like a fish.

She eats like a bird.

She sings like a bird.

Following are more expressions and their meanings in the United States. Can you add to this list?

He is a rat.
This means he is untrustworthy.

She is a turkey.
This means she is foolish and not dependable.

She is a cow.
This means she is fat and slow.

He is a pig.
This means he is dirty, messy, and vulgar.

He is a tiger.
This means watch out. He is a real fighter.

She is a fox.
This means she is pretty and sexy.

She is a snake.
This means she is untrustworthy and sly.

He is a chicken.
This means he is afraid to take action.

PRACTICE

1. Circle three of the listed comparisons with animals that you would like for someone to use when describing you.

2. Place an X beside three of the examples listed above that you hope no one will ever use to describe you.

CONVERSATION

1. If you could be an animal, which animal would you want to be? Why? What qualities do you associate with this animal?

2. Do you have a pet? What kind? If you don't have a pet now, what kind of pet would you like to have someday?

3. Have you ever been to a zoo? Which animals interested you most? If you have never been to a zoo, which animals would you like to see when you get the chance?

4. Have you ever seen animals do tricks? What did they do?

5. Is there a movie or TV show you have seen that had an animal as one of the main characters? Describe the movie. What did or didn't you like about it?

ANIMAL INSTINCT:
REVIEW OF UNIT FOUR

Match the correct expression with the meaning of the sentence.
You may look at the lessons to find your answers.

———————

_____ 1. Elephant in the room

A. No one could believe Anna won the race.

_____ 2. Like a fish out of water

B. The fancy hotel made Joe feel uncomfortable.

_____ 3. Gets my goat

C. Cheating on tests really irritated Rose.

_____ 4. Dark horse

D. It was too embarrassing to talk about it.

_____ 5. Let the cat out of the bag

E. Carlos told Juana he made the All Star team even though he had been instructed to not talk about it until it was officially announced.

UNIT FIVE
COLORFUL LANGUAGE

Bright colors are everywhere in our world. We all react to the colors around us. We also use colors in our language to describe our feelings and experiences. Using colors in our language can be fun and powerful. It is also true that how colors are expressed in our language can be confusing.

The grandmother is feeling blue because the vacation is over and her son and his family are leaving.

The traditional meaning of a color in one country may not be the same as the traditional meaning of a color in another country. For example, the color red does not mean the same in the United States as it does in China.

Also, a color can mean more than one thing within the same country. For instance, although yellow is a symbol of happy sunshine, in the United States yellow also means afraid to fight. If you say a soldier is yellow, you are actually saying he is afraid to fight.

Another example is the color green. If you say a person is green, it may mean he is concerned about nature. However, green also means inexperienced. If you say about an employee that he is green, you are saying he has not been tried or tested. He does not have enough experience.

This section is about American idioms and expressions that use colors. These idioms and expressions show what the colors mean in the United States. There is also a summary list of color clues. Have fun! I hope you are **tickled pink** with this colorful language.

25

IN THE BLACK

USAGE

"Well," said the boss to his staff, "We're finally **in the black**."

MEANING

If a business is **in the black**, it is making money. If a business is losing money, it is **in the red**.

STORY

Opening a new business is always difficult and always risky. John knew this, but he decided to take the chance anyway and buy a hardware store. He reasoned that people would be repairing their homes rather than selling their homes. He had worked in a hardware store while he was in college, and he thought he knew how to run a business. He printed flyers, placed ads, and distributed them to all the houses in the neighborhood. He ran an ad in the newspaper. He held a big opening sale to attract customers. He hired a helpful staff. Within three months, his business was **in the black**. John told his wife, "It is a relief to finally be **out of the red**. I'm so glad our business is **in the black**."

VOCABULARY

staff – a group of people working for a business or institution.

✦ *We have a staff picnic every year on July 4th.*

finally – after a long period of waiting.

✦ *Greta finally saved enough money to buy the car she wanted.*

difficult – hard; not easy.

✦ *It is difficult for children to change from one school to another.*

hardware – tools and other supplies for repair and upkeep.

✦ *Bob bought nails and paint at the hardware store.*

ads – notices to attract customers for a business or products.

✦ *The Sunday newspaper is full of good ads.*

PRACTICE

1. Decide which vocabulary word best fits the blank in each of the following sentences and write in the appropriate word.

   The teaching _____ was at the meeting to greet the parents.

   The basketball player Kobe Bryant stars in many television

   _____.

Lee asked the clerk in the _____ store which shovel was best for shoveling snow from his driveway.

2. List three ideas that would help a new business be **in the black.**

   _____

   _____

   _____

3. List three reasons why a new business might be **in the red.**

   _____

   _____

   _____

CONVERSATION

1. Would you like to own a business? What kind of business would you like to own? Why? Why not?

2. Would you rather own a business or work for someone else? What are the advantages of owning a business? What are the advantages of working for someone else?

3. What suggestions would you have for a new boss with a small staff? How should the boss treat his staff? If you were the boss, how would you treat your employees?

FEELING BLUE

USAGE

When it rains for many days, I **feel blue.**

MEANING

If someone is **feeling blue,** he is feeling sad. This is why the jazz music that expresses sadness and loss is called **the blues.**

STORY

Cindy and Paul had dated for over a year. Cindy had even hoped they might get married. Now, though, Paul had a new girlfriend, and he hadn't called Cindy for weeks. It was Valentine's Day, and that made her feel even sadder. She was sitting home alone on Valentine's Day **feeling blue.** Then she put on her favorite music and called a friend. That helped her feel a little better.

VOCABULARY

sad – a feeling of loss; a feeling of pity or self-pity; feeling down.

+ *Pablo was sad when his best friend moved to another city.*

expresses – says; symbolizes; means; tells about a feeling or idea.

+ *In America, giving someone a card with hearts on Valentine's Day expresses affection for that person.*

dated – went out together as a couple with the possibility of romance.

+ *When Joe and Megan dated, they usually went to dinner and the movies.*

hoped – wished for; wanted.

+ *Tomas and Bob hoped it would snow, so they could go sledding.*

Valentine's Day - February 14th; a holiday in America that is celebrated by exchanging cards and gifts with friends and loved ones.

+ *When Bob's class had a party on Valentine's Day, Bob gave cards to all his classmates and his teacher.*

PRACTICE

1. Read the vocabulary words and their definitions. Fill in the blanks in the following sentences with the vocabulary words that are most apt.

   It is hard to find a greeting card that really _____ feelings of love.

   My nephew was _____ when his dog died.

   I _____ Sunday would be a beautiful day for our picnic in the park.

2. Write three sentences about how you act when you **feel blue**. Do you sleep more when you **feel blue**? Do you eat more when you **feel blue**? Do you eat less? Do you exercise? Do you meditate? Do you watch TV? Write three sentences about what you do to chase away **the blues**. What helps you the most?

   _____

   _____

   _____

   _____

   _____

   _____

CONVERSATION

1. In what ways is a holiday like Valentine's Day helpful for some people? In what ways can a holiday like Valentine's Day make some people feel sad?

2. If you were the teacher for a classroom of boys and girls who were all nine years old, what would you do for a Valentine's Day party in your classroom? Would you use some art? Would you use stories? Would you talk about the history of the holiday?

Note: Red hearts are traditional for Valentine's Day.

SEE RED

USAGE

When my big brother tries to bully me, I **see red**.

MEANING

If a person **sees red**, he gets very angry.

STORY

Mrs. Jones' first grade class was playing on the playground at recess time. The playground had swings and slides and a sand box. Most of the children were taking turns and enjoying themselves. Mrs. Jones and the principal were watching the children play. When it was Stan's turn on the big slide, Jon pushed Stan aside, and Jon went down the slide first. Stan yelled at Jon, "You're not fair! You're a bully!"

Mrs. Jones said to the principal," Stan is right. When Jon acts that way, I **see red**. I just want to shake him and make him behave."

The principal said to Mrs. Jones, "Be careful. Don't let your anger get the best of you. I'll go get Jon and take him inside."

VOCABULARY

bully – a person who is cruel or unfair to others who are weaker.

> ✦ *A bully does not care about the feelings of others.*

playground – a public place near a school or park for children to play on structures like swings and slides.

> ✦ *Sarah's grandmother took her to the playground every day.*

recess – a set time during the school day for children to play.

> ✦ *If the weather is good, we go outside for recess.*

principal – a person in charge of a school.

> ✦ *A teacher may send a student to the principal for poor behavior.*

behave – act politely; act fairly; act appropriately.

> ✦ *Some children do not know how to behave in a grocery store.*

PRACTICE

1. Think about the meaning of each vocabulary word. Fill in the blank in each of the following sentences with the most apt vocabulary word.

   A _____ should be both intelligent and wise.

If you do not _____, I will punish you.

The _____ in the park had a large sand box.

2. List three things that make you **see red.**

_____

_____

_____

CONVERSATION

1. Have you ever been so angry that you really saw the color red? Why were you so angry? Did you act foolishly because you were so angry? What happened?

2. In the United States, the color red is often used as a sign to stop. When traffic lights are red, it means you should stop. Stop signs at street corners are also red. What else does the color red make you think of?

28

GREEN WITH ENVY

USAGE

When Marty saw Tom's expensive new car, he became **green with envy.**

MEANING

Green is a color associated with a wide variety of experiences. In Marty's case, green is associated with jealousy. **Green with envy** may be jealousy of another's possessions or jealousy of another's achievements. Green is the color of jealousy. Green is also the color of inexperience, as in, "He was a green recruit." Green is also associated with groups that try to protect nature.

STORY

Elaine tried very hard to be a good person. She knew she should work hard, do her best and be content with what she had. Sometimes, though, it made her sad to see others who had so much more. It especially bothered her when she did not have enough money to buy presents for her children. She was **green with envy** when her neighbors bought bicycles for their children. She wished she could give these treats to her children, too. "Someday," she said to herself. "Someday I will have what others have."

VOCABULARY

expensive – costing a lot of money; fancy.

+ *Why did you buy such an expensive watch?*

content – a feeling of satisfaction.

+ *Watching her grandchildren play in the yard, Sue felt content.*

envy – wanting what others have.

+ *Some people consider envy a green-eyed monster that turns friends into rivals.*

presents – gifts.

+ *Anna loved to buy presents for her children.*

treats – unexpected gifts; special gifts; breaks in the routine.

+ *Children receive many treats at Halloween.*

PRACTICE

1. Decide which vocabulary word best fits the blank in each of the following sentences and write in the appropriate word.

   Isaac received many _____ and _____
   for his birthday.

Buddhist monks strive to feel _____ with their lives.

_____ can destroy one's contentment with life.

2. List five things that are usually the color green.

_____   _____

_____   _____

_____

CONVERSATION

1. Have you ever felt **green with envy**? Why? Do you still feel that way?

2. The classic Greek play *Oedipus Rex* ends with the warning that you never know what a person's life will be until it's over. Everyone envied Oedipus at first, and then they realized he was really very unfortunate. Have you ever envied someone and later realized that your life was better than the life of the person you envied? Explain who, what, and why.

3. Green is also the color for the people who work to protect nature. Are you in any green groups? Do you recycle? Do you do other green activities?

> "It turned Brer Merlin green with envy and spite, which was a great satisfaction to me."
>
> ~ *A Connecticut Yankee* by Mark Twain

29

OUT OF THE BLUE

USAGE

My promotion at work came **out of the blue.**

MEANING

Out of the blue means the event was not expected.

STORY

After my brother Josh graduated from college, he went to live in New York City. While our parents were still alive, he would write or call a few times a year. He came back to town for a family reunion nine years ago, and I had not heard from Josh since then. I wrote letters to him, but my letters were returned unopened. Then last Monday, completely **out of the blue**, he showed up at my door. He had a dozen yellow roses for me in his arms, and a big smile on his face. I couldn't believe it. He really surprised me. I was so glad to see him. We talked for hours. I hope we never again lose touch.

VOCABULARY

graduated – met the requirements and received a degree.

✦ *My parents were pleased when I graduated with honors.*

parents – mother and father; mom and dad.

✦ *Shannon's parents paid for all her college expenses.*

unopened – still closed; still sealed; not opened.

✦ *The unopened envelope had no return address.*

dozen – twelve.

✦ *Bob buys one dozen bagels from the bakery every Sunday.*

lose touch – fail to keep in contact over a period of time; fail to keep in touch or stay in touch.

✦ *Many people lose touch with their childhood friends.*

PRACTICE

1. Fill in the blanks in the following sentences with the appropriate words from the vocabulary list.
   Anne's _____ insisted that she finish her
   homework before she could watch television.

   There are at least a _____ reasons why you
   should stop smoking cigarettes.

Jan said to his college roommate, "Be sure to not
_____."

2. Write a sentence about something that happened to **you out of the blue.**

_____

_____

CONVERSATION

1. Sometimes it is fun to try to figure out how expressions started. How do you think the expression **out of the blue** came about? Use your imagination. Make up a story. There is no wrong answer.

2. What is your favorite color? What feeling does this color give you? Do you have any special associations with this color? Which color do most people in your class prefer?

> "One can't impose unity out of the blue on a country that has 265 different kinds of cheese."
>
> *Charles DeGaulle (1890-1970), French General and President*

TICKLED PINK

USAGE

Brenda was **tickled pink** with her new hairdo.

MEANING

If someone is **tickled pink**, she is very happy and smiling.

STORY

The big day had arrived. Yuni was graduating from college. She had worked hard for four years, and now she had a degree in elementary education. She even had a job for the fall. She would be teaching first grade at the local school. During the summer, she planned to take a vacation. After she returned, she would move out of her parents' home and get an apartment. Everything was just great. She was **tickled pink** with her graduation and all her plans for the future. Her parents, too, were happy for her success.

VOCABULARY

tickled - caused to laugh.

> ✦ *It tickled Ben to see his baby sister try to walk.*

degree - a certificate of achievement from a college.

> ✦ *John's BA degree in philosophy was no guarantee of a job.*

local - in the nearby area; in the surrounding neighborhood.

> ✦ *My local grocery store has very fresh tomatoes in the summer.*

apartment - a unit to live in that has one or more rooms and is part of a larger building.

> ✦ *The large, older home had been divided into three apartments.*

future - a time that has not yet come; tomorrow and more.

> ✦ *No one can really know what the future will be.*

PRACTICE

1. Read the vocabulary words, their definitions, and the example sentences. Then fill in the blanks in the following sentences with the appropriate words from the vocabulary list.

   The _____ bus only runs once an hour.

Will people from earth live on Mars in the _____?

A larger _____ is more expensive, but I need the space.

2. Think about the word **tickled**. Has anyone ever **tickled** your feet? Are you very **ticklish**? Do you like to be physically **tickled**? Has anyone ever told a joke that **tickled** you? Have you ever seen something that **tickled** you? Write three sentences using either the word **tickled** or the expression **tickled pink**.

_____

_____

_____

_____

_____

_____

CONVERSATION

1. It may be that the expression **tickled pink** comes from the fact that some people blush or turn pink when they are happy. The expression that **life is rosy** probably comes from the same fact that some people blush when they are happy. When **life is rosy**, things seem very good. Do you ever blush? Is it always from happiness? Is your future **rosy** now? Are you **tickled pink** about your future? Why or why not.

2. What three things do you think will change in the future? Will people be happier when these changes happen?

3. In the United States, the color pink is associated with baby girls. If a baby is wrapped in a pink blanket, the baby is probably a girl. Do you have other associations with the color pink?

> "If I can put one touch of rosy sunset into the life of any man or woman, I shall feel that I have worked with God."
>
> *G.K. Chesterton (1874-1936), English writer and journalist*

COLOR CLUES

This short guide to color meanings in the United States may be helpful. Since all colors have a variety of meanings, you must always look at the context. For example, blue is the color associated with baby boys, but feeling blue means feeling sad. The other words in the sentence will help you know which meaning is intended.

Blue is the traditional color for gifts for baby boys.

If a person is feeling **blue**, he is sad.

If a business is in the **red**, it is losing money.

Red on a traffic light or sign means stop.

If a person is seeing **red**, he is very angry.

If a person is caught **red-handed**, he is caught doing something wrong.

If a person is called **yellow**, it is being said that he is afraid to fight.

Yellow on a traffic light or sign means caution.

Green on a traffic light means go.

If a person is **green**, he is trying to protect nature.

If a person is called **green** at a job or activity, he has no experience.

If a person is **green** with envy, he is jealous.

If a person is tickled **pink**, she is very pleased.

Pink is the traditional color for gifts for baby girls.

Purple is the traditional color for royalty.

White is the traditional color for a bride to wear at her wedding.

To wave a **white** flag means to surrender.

If something is **black and white**, it is very clear with a definite contrast.

Black is the traditional color to wear at funerals.

If a business is in the **black**, it is making money and profitable.

DO YOU KNOW YOUR COLORS?

Using the color clues in this unit, fill in the blank in each of the following sentences with the appropriate color. A color may be used more than once.

I bought a _____ blanket for my baby granddaughter.

John was happy because his business was finally in the
_____.

When I saw the _____ traffic light, I knew I had to stop.

Ida wore a _____ suit to her mother's funeral as a sign of respect.

When Charles yelled at her for no reason, Kathy saw _____.

The queen wore a _____ robe with white fur trim.

The bride wore a traditional _____ gown with a veil and long train.

I bought a _____ blanket for my baby grandson.

When my new car was delivered, I was tickled _____.

I knew my next door neighbor was _____ with envy.

The _____ movement works to protect our oceans, lakes, and rivers.

COLORFUL COMMENTS:
REVIEW OF UNIT FIVE

Match the correct expression with the meaning of the sentence.

_____

_____ 1. John was pleased his business made a profit.

A. See red

_____ 2. Juana was sad her father moved to Phoenix.

B. Green with envy

_____ 3. Isabella got angry when Paulo forgot their anniversary.

C. In the black

_____ 4. Jose was jealous when he saw Carlos drive up in his new Ferrari.

D. Out of the Blue

_____ 5. Aba could not believe his aunt showed up unannounced from Kenya.

E. Tickled pink

_____ 6. Kim was overjoyed when Tuan asked her to marry him.

F. Feeling blue

UNIT SIX
HOW'S THE WEATHER?

Many common expressions use words that relate to weather or temperature. Since we all share weather and temperature conditions, they are easy to talk about. Often the first thing strangers talk about is the weather. How many times have you started a conversation with, "Oh, isn't this a beautiful day?" or "I wonder how much longer this rain will last?" Words that describe weather or temperature are part of our basic vocabulary. They express shared experiences.

The boy is enjoying his snowman.
Is this how the idiom "chill out" started?

Sometimes expressions that use weather or temperature terms are easy to understand. If one knows the word fog, it is easy to understand that the expression **walking around in a fog** means being unaware of one's surroundings or having no clue what one is doing.

If one knows that the word lukewarm means neither hot nor cold, it is easy to understand that if one is **lukewarm to an idea**, it means one is neither strongly for it nor strongly against it.

Sometimes, though, idioms that use weather or temperature words are not obvious. What does it mean to feel **under the weather**? What is a **fair weather friend**? This section contains some common expressions that relate to the weather or temperature.

So relax. They're fun. **It's a breeze!**

31

UNDER THE WEATHER

USAGE

David said he's not coming in to work today because he is feeling **under the weather**.

MEANING

If a person is **under the weather**, he is not feeling as good as usual. Maybe he is tired. Maybe he is a little sick. Maybe he just feels sad. He is not seriously ill or in crisis. He is just a little **under the weather**.

STORY

My friend Sally is a kindergarten teacher. She is usually a very cheerful person. We laugh a lot when we are together. She tells me stories about the funny things the little children do or say in her classroom. When we met after work yesterday, though, she seemed quiet and a little sad. I said, Sally, are you feeling okay? Is something the matter?

Sally said, "Oh, no. I'm just a little **under the weather**."

VOCABULARY

weather – the condition of the atmosphere regarding temperature, moisture, wind, and pressure.

✦ *Felix loves to go jogging in warm, sunny weather.*

crisis – a very difficult situation; a breakdown.

✦ *It is often a crisis for children if their parents get divorced.*

kindergarten – a school for children who are approximately five years old.

✦ *Children in kindergarten learn the letters in the alphabet, do arts and crafts, learn numbers, and play games.*

cheerful – full of cheer; feeling joyful; smiling and positive.

✦ *Nick likes to play games with his cheerful uncle.*

yesterday – the day immediately before today.

✦ *Yesterday I had a little headache, but today I feel fine.*

PRACTICE

1. Look again at the vocabulary words. Fill in the blanks in the following sentences with the vocabulary words that best fit the meaning.

   I'm sorry for what I said to you _____.

Don stayed calm during the _____ when others panicked.

The TV host was always smiling and _____.

2. Read each of the following questions about the weather. Circle either *Yes* or *No* to show your answer.

Do you like cold weather?
Yes / No

Do you like hot weather?
Yes / No

Do you like rainy weather?
Yes / No

Do you like snow?
Yes / No

CONVERSATION

1. When you feel **under the weather**, what do you do to feel better? Do you go for a walk? Do you call a friend? Do you eat or drink something special?

2. Did you go to a kindergarten? How old were you? Did you like it? What activities did you do?

3. Which time of year do you like best? What do you do during your favorite season?

RAINING CATS AND DOGS

USAGE

It was **raining cats and dogs** when we were driving to the airport.

MEANING

If it is **raining cats and dogs**, it is raining very heavily.

STORY

Felipe and Maria decided to go to the movies in New York City. They felt lucky when they found a free and legal parking place three blocks from the theater. After the movie was over, though, it was **raining cats and dogs**. Felipe said, "Oh no, I forgot my umbrella. There is no sense in both of us getting wet. Maria, you wait here in the lobby while I get the car." Even though Felipe ran to the car, he got soaked in the downpour. When Felipe returned with the car to the theater, Maria thought she had a very **cool** boyfriend.

VOCABULARY

free – at no cost.

+ *Ever since Clara could remember, the beach was free and for the public.*

legal – within the law; not against the law.

+ *In many states, the legal age to get a learner's permit to drive is sixteen.*

soaked – completely wet; thoroughly wet; getting drenched.

+ *The chef soaked the chicken in his favorite sauce.*

downpour – a very heavy rain.

+ *Bill got soaked in the downpour.*

umbrella – a handheld protection against rain.

+ *People who live in London often take an umbrella in case it rains.*

PRACTICE

1. Fill in each of the blanks in the following sentences with the most apt vocabulary word.

   The _____ speed limit on highways in Texas has been raised to 80 miles per hour.

Even though Karen used a large umbrella, she got
_____ in the downpour.

The ad said, "Buy one can of peaches, get one _____."

2. The word *downpour* is a compound word. A compound word is made by joining two words. In this case, the word *down* and the word *pour* have been joined to form the word *downpour*. Read the following words and circle those that are compound words.

thing	somewhere	grocery	smartphone
something	chocolate	eyeglasses	underground
hand	basketball	family	childbirth
handbag	pancake	computer	bookstore
rain	snowball	earring	washrag
raining	surprise	fingernail	racehorse
raincoat	dollhouse	lawyer	eyeball

CONVERSATION

1. Who are your favorite movie stars? Why?
2. Would you like to be a movie star? Why or why not?
3. Do you like animated movies? Which is your favorite animated movie?
4. Do you remember the first movie you ever saw? What was it?

FAIR WEATHER FRIEND

USAGE

Alice said Janice was a **fair weather friend** since she always seemed to disappear when trouble came.

MEANING

A **fair weather friend** is one who is a friend only when life is easy. A **fair weather friend** does not offer help or comfort when life is difficult.

STORY

Alice and Janice went to high school together. They enjoyed chatting with each other. They shared the same taste in music and movies. They laughed a lot when they were together. Then, Alice's father had a fatal heart attack. Alice phoned Janice, but she couldn't reach her. Alice left a message, but Janice did not call her back. When Alice returned to school, Janice avoided her. Alice felt confused and betrayed. She thought, "I guess she was not my friend after all. I guess Janice was just a **fair weather friend.**"

VOCABULARY

chatting – talking easily back and forth.

> ✦ *The two young mothers were sitting on a park bench and chatting about their babies.*

taste – an appreciation for a certain style; one's likes and dislikes.

> ✦ *Leah does not share Gil's practical taste in clothes.*

fatal – resulting in death.

> ✦ *We were relieved when the doctor said the injury was not fatal.*

confused – a feeling of uncertainty; an unsure feeling.

> ✦ *The signs on the highway confused me.*

betrayed – a feeling that one has been treated unfairly and cruelly by a friend, a family member, or a fellow worker.

> ✦ *Julius Caesar felt betrayed when Brutus stabbed him.*

PRACTICE

1. Fill in the blanks in the following sentences with the most appropriate words from your vocabulary list.

   The girl at the bus stop was _____ loudly on her cell phone.

Joe's favorite movie is _____ Attraction.

When you told my secret to Anna, you _____ me.

2. Use the expression **fair weather friend** in a sentence.

_____

_____

CONVERSATION

1. Chat with others about your taste in music. What do you like? What don't you like?

2. Chat with others about your taste in clothes. Are you a fashionable person?

3. Chat with others about your taste in movies. What are your favorite movies? Are you turned off by violence? Do you like to see movies from other countries? Do you like to see movies in other languages?

Other choices: During the American Revolution for freedom, the writer Thomas Paine wrote about "the summer soldier and the sunshine patriot." Paine was describing those who fought only when the weather was easy, but quit fighting when the weather was cold and food supplies were low. Paine was telling the soldiers to not be **fair weather friends.**

CHILL OUT / BE COOL

USAGE

Teenagers often **chill out** at the local mall.
"Sue, **chill out**, we'll get there in time."

MEANING

Chill out means to relax and be at ease. **Chill out** means to have no particular plan in mind. **Chill out** or **be cool** can also be used to tell people to relax or to lose their impatience or anger.

STORY

On Saturdays Ian usually went to the mall to hang out with his friends. Lots of teenagers met there each week. They were just **chilling out**, teasing each other and telling stories. James often had to work on Saturdays, so he wasn't often able to join them. One Saturday, though, his shift did not start until 6 p.m., so he went to the mall to join his friends. When James got there, he saw his girlfriend May flirting with Ian. He became furious. James went up to Ian and shoved him. Ian said, "Hey, **chill out**. We were just playing. I know she's your girl. **Be cool**."

VOCABULARY

relax – not to be tense; to be at ease; to be casual.

    ✦ *In order to relax after work, Jim shot baskets with his buddies.*

mall – an area with many stores, often enclosed under one roof.

    ✦ *It is convenient to go to the mall to buy presents for family and friends.*

shift (at work) – a set sequence of hours to work, such as 8 a.m. to 4 p.m., 4 p.m. to 12 a.m., or 12 a.m. to 8 a.m.

    ✦ *The shift from 12 a.m.-8 a.m. is called the graveyard shift.*

furious – very angry.

    ✦ *When Sue lied about me to our friends, I was furious.*

shoved – pushed forcefully.

    ✦ *Gwen shoved through the crowd to get Brad Pitt's autograph.*

PRACTICE

1. Fill in the blanks in the following sentences with the appropriate words from the vocabulary list.

   On the weekend, I try to _____ and forget work.

Jan was _____ with Steve when he forgot their date.

Some people prefer the night _____ because it is calmer.

2. Some people count to ten when they need to **chill out**. Some people just walk away from trouble when they need to **chill out**. Write a sentence about what you do when you need to calm down.

_____

_____

CONVERSATION

1. What do you and your friends do when you want to just **chill out**? Where do you go?

2. Do boys and girls these days usually hang out together? Do they go to parties together or meet at a common place?

> "Nothing gives one person so much advantage over another as to remain always cool ... under all circumstances."
>
> *Thomas Jefferson (1743-1826),*
> *Founding Father and 3rd President of the United States*

IN HOT WATER

USAGE

Tom forgot his wedding anniversary, and now he is **in hot water** with his wife.

MEANING

If a person is **in hot water**, he is in trouble. He has made problems for himself and others. His own actions have gotten him into trouble. Someone is angry with him and is giving him a hard time. Perhaps he forgot a deadline at work and is now **in hot water** with his boss. Perhaps he forgot his wedding anniversary and now is **in hot water** with his wife. Perhaps he did not pay his taxes, and now he is **in hot water** with the government. If a person is **in hot water**, he is in trouble.

STORY

Jane bought two theater tickets to a play she really wanted to see. Good seats cost more than she thought they would, but she bought them anyway. She really wanted to see this play. She asked her boyfriend Mark if he would like to go with her, and he said, "Sure. That would be great!" When Saturday came, Mark played football in the park with his buddies. Then the guys went to a bar for a few beers. A good football game was playing on the television. The friends sat around cheering and joking. Mark completely forgot about his plans with Jane. When he did not come on time, Jane tried to call him, but the bar was so noisy, he did not hear the phone ring. Mark forgot their date. Jane did not see the play. Now, each time he calls, she hangs up on him. Mark is really **in hot water.**

VOCABULARY

play – drama; a live presentation with characters and a story.

+ *The play was about a son who had problems with his parents.*

theater – the space in which a play is performed.

+ *Anton prefers a small theater for serious plays.*

anniversary – the date on which something special happened.

+ *Tim's and Josie's wedding anniversary was on June 19th.*

buddies – pals; friends with whom one spends a lot of time.

+ *John and Paul had been best buddies since first grade.*

noisy – full of noise; loud and confusing.

+ *The subway was so noisy that Isabella could not hear her phone ring.*

PRACTICE

1. Fill in each blank in the following sentences with the most appropriate vocabulary word from your list.

   Hamlet is a famous _____ by Shakespeare.

   The boys were so _____ that they gave their mom a headache.

   My _____ and I took a road trip to Florida.

2. Write a sentence using the idiom **in hot water**.

   _____

   _____

CONVERSATION

1. In the story, why was Jane so angry? How would you feel if you were in her situation? Would you ever forgive Mark? Are you still angry about something that happened years ago? What happened? Will your feelings ever change?

2. Have you ever seen a play? Where? Were you ever in a play? Did you enjoy the experience? Is there a play you would recommend to others?

Other choices: Another idiom that means the same as **in hot water** is **in the doghouse.** One could say Mark is **in hot water** or one could say Mark is **in the doghouse.**

> "Women are like teabags. We don't know our true strength until we are in hot water."
>
> *Eleanor Roosevelt (1884-1962), Humanitarian and First Lady of the United States*

HOT TIME

The main meaning of the word **hot** is high in temperature. The word **hot** also has many other meanings in informal English. This list contains some other common usages.

Hot = spicy.
*Indian restaurants often will fix dishes as **hot** or mild.*

Hot = currently popular.
*A few years ago, Tickle Me Elmo was a **hot** toy at Christmas.*

Hot = sexy
*Many movie fans think Angelina Jolie is **hot**.*

Hot under the collar = angry.
*When his secretary lost the paperwork for the sale, the boss was **hot under the collar**.*

Hot streak = a series of wins in sports.
*The Chicago Bears were on a **hot streak**.*

Hot potato = a disturbing topic, something one wants to get rid of as quickly as possible.
*The topic of abortion is a **hot potato** in our family.*

Hot hand = the ability to score many points in a game.
*Chris Paul had a **hot hand** during the basketball play-offs.*

Hotshot = someone with a big ego who brags on himself.
*A **hotshot** is seldom a good team player.*

WEATHER REPORT: REVIEW OF UNIT SIX

Match the expression with the meaning. You may look at the lessons.

_____

_____ 1. The team had won twenty games in a row.

_____ 2. Richard was very angry.

_____ 3. Susie was not feeling as well as usual.

_____ 4. The friends often met at the mall.

_____ 5. Sam told Bob to relax.

_____ 6. Carla was never there when I needed her.

_____ 7. There was a heavy downpour.

A. She felt **under the weather**.

B. It was **raining cats and dogs**.

C. He said to **be cool**.

D. She is a **fair weather friend**.

E. They liked to **chill out** together.

F. They were on a **hot streak**.

G. He was **hot under the collar**.

UNIT SEVEN
WHERE ARE YOU?

Where are you? When we ask this question, we may mean many things. Perhaps we are asking where you are physically. The answer to that question is usually easy. You may be at home. You may be at school. You may be at the store. Answering with a physical location is usually easy.

You can't move if you're stuck between a rock and a hard place.

But what if the question means where are you psychologically? What if the question means where are you emotionally? What if the question means where do you stand on an issue? Then the question is often difficult to answer.

That is when the idioms in this unit are useful. By using descriptions of physical locations, these idioms are describing the location of a person's thoughts or feelings. For example, if one is undecided, the expression that describes that state of mind is **sitting on a fence**. This is a physical location that creates a clear picture. This image shows the mental state of undecided.

Another example is **down in the dumps**. This is a physical location that describes a feeling of sadness. This unit contains many more examples. The idea may be difficult to explain, but the idioms are easy. That is their job. They are making communication easier.

SITTING ON THE FENCE

USAGE

Although the election is next week, Mary is still sitting on the fence. Who would make the best governor?

MEANING

If one is **sitting on the fence**, he hasn't decided which way to go. One is not yet committed, meaning he hasn't jumped down from the fence to one side or the other. One is **sitting on the fence**.

STORY

The presidential election was only one week away. Mary's parents were going to vote for the Democratic candidate, but her husband was voting for an independent candidate as a protest vote. Whenever her parents and her husband got together, they argued about the coming election. Mary listened to both sides, and she couldn't decide which way to vote. Mary was still **sitting on the fence**.

VOCABULARY

fence – a long, thin, upright barrier used to mark boundaries.

+ *The dog was able to dig beneath the fence and get into the neighbor's yard.*

decide – choose; make a decision.

+ *I can't decide if I want cheesecake or carrot cake for dessert.*

committed – strongly supporting.

+ *I am committed to losing ten pounds before my birthday.*

election – the process of voting for a candidate; the process by which the person who gets the most votes wins the position.

+ *The elections for government offices in the United States are usually held the first Tuesday in November.*

independent – not associated with a major political party.

+ *In the United States, independent candidates seldom win elections.*

PRACTICE

1. Fill in each blank with the vocabulary word that best completes the meaning of each sentence.

   We built a tall _____ in our back yard.

I am _____ to my husband and my children.

It is unusual when an independent candidate wins the

_____.

2. Write a sentence that uses the expression **sitting on the fence.**

_____

_____

CONVERSATION

1. Describe a situation in which you were **sitting on the fence.** Did you decide correctly?

2. Did you ever build a fence? What was it made of? Why did you build it?

3. A common saying is: "Good fences make good neighbors." What does this saying mean? Do you agree? Do you disagree? Why?

OUT ON A LIMB

USAGE

The basketball coach went **out on a limb** and said with confidence that his team would win the play-offs.

MEANING

If a person goes **out on a limb**, he is stating that he will do something difficult. He is risking his reputation just like a person who climbs out on the end of a tree limb is risking his safety. The limb might break. He might fall. If he is not careful, he might get hurt. If a person fails to do what he has said he will do, his reputation will get hurt. It is risky to go **out on a limb**.

STORY

The professional basketball season was almost over. Only two teams were left in the competition: the Miami Heat and the Los Angeles Lakers. LeBron James was very confident that his team would win. He told the reporters, "I guarantee that we will be the champs."

One reporter said, "You're really **going out on a limb**. The Lakers have a better record this season than the Heat."

LeBron replied, "I am **going out on a limb**, but I know we will win this series, and we will win the championship."

VOCABULARY

limb – the branch of a tree; a person's arm or leg.

✦ *A limb of the oak tree fell down in the storm last night.*

risk – a chance; to take a chance; to make a gamble.

✦ *He took a risk when he invested his savings in stocks.*

coach – a teacher of skills for a game.

✦ *Most Boston Celtics fans agree that Doc Rivers is a great coach.*

guarantee – to be absolutely positive; to provide assurance.

✦ *Used cars that are bought from a dealer usually have a six-month guarantee.*

record – a statement of wins and losses; a collection of facts.

✦ *The politician said, "I'm proud of my accomplishments. Look at my record."*

PRACTICE

1. Write a sentence using the idiom **out on a limb** correctly. The context of your sentence should show your understanding of the idiom **out on a limb**.

_____

_____

2. Use one of the vocabulary words to correctly fill in the blank in each of the following sentences.

For many years, basketball star Reggie Miller held the _____ for the total number of three point baskets.

One _____ of the tree was dead, but the others were all healthy.

The salesman said, "Buying these stocks is not a _____, but rather a wise investment for years to come.

CONVERSATION

1. Can you think of an example when someone went **out on a limb** and was successful?

2. Can you think of an example when someone went **out on a limb** and his prediction was not successful?

3. How does it make you feel when you trust someone's words and then it doesn't happen as he said it would?

38

UP IN THE AIR

USAGE

Their wedding plans were **up in the air**.

MEANING

If a plan is **up in the air**, it is undecided. It is unclear. It has no shape. It is cloudy. **Up in the air** is the opposite of grounded and practical.

STORY

Joyce and Mike were engaged to be married. They were very much in love, but they had different visions for their wedding. Joyce wanted a large church wedding, with all their family and friends there. Mike wanted the two of them to elope. When Joyce's mother asked about their wedding plans, Joyce said, "I have no idea. Nothing is decided. It's all **up in the air**."

VOCABULARY

___

vague – unclear; without detail; uninformed.

+ *I have a vague idea about how a plane can fly.*

engaged – promised in marriage.

+ *Alicia and Scott were engaged for two years before they got married.*

elope – marry in secret; run away to get married.

+ *Often parents are disappointed if their child elopes.*

grounded – practical; realistic; knowledgeable.

+ *A fireman should be well grounded in methods of fire prevention.*

vision – a picture; an idea of a future event.

+ *Her vision for their future included having four children.*

PRACTICE

___

1. Fill in each of the blanks in the following sentences with the most appropriate vocabulary word.

   Jane has a practical, _____ plan for improving sales.
   On the other hand, John's ideas are _____ and unclear.

Many prophets reported they experienced a _____.

2. Write your own sentence showing the correct use of the phrase **up in the air** in your sentence.

_____

_____

3. List other words in the lesson that are new to you. Can you guess the meaning of these words? Use a dictionary to define the words. Were your guesses close to the correct meanings?

_____   _____

_____   _____

_____

CONVERSATION

1. Do you think people should get married if their parents disapprove?

2. Who do you think should plan a wedding?

3. Who do you think should pay for a wedding? Does the age of the couple getting married make a difference in your answer?

DOWN IN THE DUMPS

USAGE

When Fred cancelled his plans to come visit her, Angela felt **down in the dumps.**

MEANING

If one is **down in the dumps,** one is sad. If one is **down in the dumps,** one is feeling low. Feeling **down in the dumps** is a mood that lasts for a while; it is not just the feeling of a moment.

STORY

Angela was excited because her brother Fred was coming home for a visit. She wanted to show him the new sports stadium in town. She wanted to introduce him to her friends. She wanted to talk with him like they did when they were younger. Then, just three days before he had planned to come home, he broke his leg. He called Angela from the hospital and said, "Sorry, Angie, I just can't make it. I promise I'll come home in a few months." Of course, Angela knew Fred could no longer make the trip. She tried to sound cheerful when he called, but she was very disappointed. Angela felt really **down in the dumps.**

VOCABULARY

cancel – back out of a plan; decide against a plan.

+ *Jane decided to cancel her newspaper subscription.*

stadium – a large facility used for sporting events or concerts.

+ *The new stadium held twice as many people as the old one.*

introduce – to present one person to another; to bring in a new idea.

+ *Bill asked Marie, "When will you introduce me to your family?"*

hospital – a facility with medical staff and equipment.

+ *The emergency room at the hospital is usually crowded.*

ruined – no longer usable; no longer workable.

+ *When Joe spilled coffee on Frank, Frank's jacket was ruined.*

PRACTICE

1. Review the vocabulary words. Fill in each blank in the following sentences with the vocabulary word that best fits the meaning of the sentence.

   Betty took her dog to the animal _____ when it was sick.

The teenage girl said to her mother, "You have _____ my life."

We bought season football tickets when the new _____ was completed.

2. Answer each of the following questions:

Have you ever felt **down in the dumps?** _____

How long did your mood last? _____

What did you do to help yourself feel better?

_____

_____

CONVERSATION

1. What suggestions can you give to someone who feels **down in the dumps** to help him or her feel better? Does exercise help you when you are **down in the dumps?** Is there a special food that helps you when you are **down in the dumps?**

2. Do you have brothers or sisters? How close are you in age? What do you enjoy doing together? Do you live in a different place from any of your brothers or sisters? Has this changed your relationship? Do you get together for any holidays? Do you have family reunions?

Other choices: See the expression **feeling blue. Feeling blue** is like being **down in the dumps.** They are both expressions that mean feeling sad.

40

BETWEEN A ROCK AND A HARD PLACE

USAGE

Jonah was out of time. He had to choose between catching a later plane or going on vacation without any clothes. He was **between a rock and a hard place.**

MEANING

If one is **between a rock and a hard place**, one is trapped between two bad choices. In other words, there is no good option.

STORY

Karl believed it was his duty as a citizen to vote. He read all the information he could about the candidates. This time he was having a hard time: he did not like either one of them. One said the right things, but he was known to be dishonest. The second candidate seemed honest, but uninformed. For whom should he vote? Karl felt he was trapped **between a rock and a hard place.**

VOCABULARY

option – choice, selection.

> ✦ *You have the option of returning your merchandise within a week free of charge if it is unsatisfactory.*

citizen – a person with legal status in a country.

> ✦ *After passing the citizenship test, the immigrant was sworn in as a citizen on July 4th, 2011.*

trapped – caught in a trap; cornered; having no way out.

> ✦ *The robber was trapped in the alley by the police.*

dishonest – not honest; hypocritical; untrustworthy.

> ✦ *The newspaper reported that the candidate made dishonest deals with his big business supporters.*

uninformed – unaware; without the true facts.

> ✦ *If one is uninformed, he can easily be misled.*

PRACTICE

1. Write in the blank the vocabulary word that best completes the meaning of the sentence.

   A person cannot vote in the United States presidential election if he is not a _____ of the United States.

If I won the lottery, I would choose the _____ of $50,000 each year rather than $500,000 all at once.

Firemen learn how to save people who are _____ in burning buildings.

2. In addition to a rock, list five objects that are hard.

_____   _____

_____   _____

_____

CONVERSATION

1. What are the qualities that you look for in a candidate? Why?

2. Have you ever felt that you were trapped between **a rock and a hard place**? Explain the situation. What happened? Would you make the same decision if you had the chance to do it over again?

OUT OF THE LOOP

USAGE

Why am I suddenly being left **out of the loop**?

MEANING

If one is **out of the loop,** he or she is no longer being included in a group. If one is **out of the loop,** one is no longer receiving invitations and information from those in the "in" group. A person can be **out of the loop** at work or **out of the loop** with a social group.

STORY

Andrew had been an assistant manager in the advertising division for three years. When the advertising manager retired, Andrew expected that he would get that job. Then one day he noticed that everyone else in the advertising division was meeting in the board room. He said to his secretary, "Did I get a memo about a meeting? What's happening? Why am I **out of the loop?**"

VOCABULARY

---

loop – a circle.

> ✦ *The cowboy made a loop on his rope.*

assistant – helper; one being trained for a higher position.

> ✦ *Robert had been the assistant bank manager for two years.*

division – a section of a larger company, such as sales, advertising, etc.

> ✦ *Nate started in the accounting division, but then he transferred to the sales division and made more money.*

executive – among the top positions in a company.

> ✦ *Sarah Johnson was the chief executive officer of the company.*

memo – memorandum; a short note from one person to others in the same business.

> ✦ *All the teachers received a memo from the principal about a required meeting after school in the library.*

PRACTICE

---

1. Fill in the blank in each of the following sentences with the most fitting word from your vocabulary list.

As soon as Carl received the _____, he called his boss.

People in the sales _____ usually make more money than those in shipping.

The _____ was given a $1,000,000 bonus by the board.

2. The word *memo* is used in daily speech. It is short for memorandum. Each of the following words also has a shortened form that is used in daily speech. Write the informal form in the blank beside the word. See the example.

memorandum: **memo**

gymnasium: _____

telephone: _____

television: _____

automobile: _____

bicycle: _____

CONVERSATION

1. Have you ever felt left **out of the loop**? Have you ever felt left out by a group of friends? What happened? Did you ever feel **out of the loop** at school? What happened? Did you ever feel **out of the loop** at a job? Why did you feel that way?

2. Have you ever decided to "drop" someone from your group of friends? Why did you drop that person? Did you tell the person? Did you just stop talking to the person? What happened?

3. Do you use social media like Facebook? How many Facebook friends do you have? What is the difference between the way you talk with your Facebook friends and the way you talk with your close friends?

42

FLYING UNDER THE RADAR

USAGE

I was **flying under the radar** at work until I could finish the yearly report that was overdue.

MEANING

If one is **flying under the radar**, one is trying to avoid attention. If one is **flying under the radar**, one is hoping no one will notice.

STORY

Aimee had tried out for a small part in the school play. She was so busy with her homework and her job that she had not learned her lines before the first rehearsal. She said to her friend Tony, "I hope the director doesn't rehearse my scene tonight. If I can be quiet tonight, I will learn my lines by tomorrow night's rehearsal. I hope that for one night, I can **fly under the radar**."

VOCABULARY

___

radar – a way to detect an object's position or speed by radio waves.

   ✦ *The airport controller saw a UFO, an unidentified flying object, on his radar.*

attention – close or careful notice.

   ✦ *Han waved and tried to get Lee's attention across the street.*

rehearsal – a practice for a performance.

   ✦ *The director scheduled a rehearsal for Act I at 7 p.m.*

director – the person in charge of a performance or production.

   ✦ *George Clooney is both an actor and a director.*

scene – a part of an act in a play; a view in one place and time.

   ✦ *They practiced the fight scene again and again until it looked real enough to film.*

PRACTICE

___

1. Fill in each of the blanks in the following sentences with the most apt vocabulary word.

   Bob got his _____ technician training in the army.

Ang Lee won the Academy Award for best _____.

The play had completely captured the audience's

_____.

2. The word radar is a palindrome. A palindrome is a word that is spelled the same backwards and forwards. Can you list four more English palindromes?

_____   _____

_____   _____

CONVERSATION

1. What are some tips for someone who is trying to **fly under the radar**. For example, if one is trying to **fly under the radar**, how should one dress? How should one sit? What about eye contact?

2. Have you ever tried to **fly under the radar** in the classroom? Why? Were you successful? What happened?

3. Did you ever try to **fly under the radar** with your parents? Why? Were you successful? What happened?

Note: Radar is an acronym for radio detecting and ranging.

HERE YOU ARE:
REVIEW OF UNIT SEVEN

Match the idiom with the corresponding sentence.

_____

_____ 1. Meagan was hoping the teacher would not call on her since she had not prepared for class.

A. He was **between a rock and a hard place.**

_____ 2. Cindy had no idea where she would go for her vacation.

B. She was **sitting on the fence.**

_____ 3. I am betting all my money on an unknown horse in the third race.

C. I am going **out on a limb.**

_____ 4. Gigi couldn't decide which candidate she should support.

D. He was **out of the loop.**

_____ 5. Alex was surprised that he had not been invited to the party.

E. She was **flying under the radar.**

_____ 6. Max had to either lose his job or take a large cut in salary.

F. She was **down in the dumps.**

_____ 7. Sarah felt sad all day.

G. Her plans were **up in the air.**

DO YOU REALLY KNOW
YOUR IDIOMS?

Match the idiom with the corresponding sentence.

————

____ 1. Sal thought the final exam was *so* easy.

A. Raining cats and dogs

____ 2. Roberto loved to play jokes on Carlos.

B. Piece of cake

____ 3. Nobody expected Little Sunshine to win the race.

C. Toot their own horn

____ 4. Jose watches at least five hours of television every day.

D. Couch potato

____ 5. When Clara came home at 2:00 AM, she knew she'd be in trouble.

E. Pulling my leg

____ 6. One day before the election, John still hadn't decided whom to vote for.

F. Dark horse

____ 7. Joe and Pete love to talk and go to the movies together.

G. In hot water

_____ 8. Janice got all wet in the tropical storm.

H. Sitting on the fence

_____ 9. Olga showed Bob everything he needed to know to manage the store.

I. Chill out

_____ 10. Susan had a slight headache and really wasn't feeling well.

J. Learn the ropes

_____ 11. Joyce thought the two masked men running down the alley were up to no good.

K. Under the weather

_____ 12. The two young men did not call the police when they saw the old man being robbed.

L. Something is fishy

_____ 13. Sam didn't know if he would get the job.

M. Turned a blind eye

_____ 14. Athletes and politicians enjoy talking about their accomplishments.

N. Up in the air

INDEX OF IDIOMS
AND EXPRESSIONS

(Expressions in bold are featured in this book)

A

A bad egg – a bad person; a person who brings trouble.

A chicken – a person who is afraid to fight or take action.

A cow – a person who is fat and slow.

A fox – a person who is sly or sneaky.

A fox – a female who is attractive and sexy.

A pain in the neck – a bother; a pest.

A peach – a wonderful person.

A piece of cake – easy.

A pig – a person who is dirty, messy, disgusting.

A rat – a person who is untrustworthy; one who betrays friends or coworkers.

A snake – a person who is sneaky and untrustworthy.

A stick in the mud – a person who is unavailable for fun or change.

A turkey – a person who is foolish and out of step; a jerk.

B

Be cool - relax; take it easy; do not be angry.

Between a rock and a hard place – having an option between two bad choices.

Brings home the bacon – earns money to support a family.

Broad shoulders – the ability to assume responsibility or take criticism.

Brush someone off – ignore someone; drop someone's acquaintance.

Bucket list – a list of actions one wants to do at sometime.

Bump up – make more interesting.

C

Chill out – be cool; relax with friends; lose one's anger.

Cold shoulder – ignore someone.

Cost an arm and a leg – is very expensive.

Couch potato – an inactive person who watches television for many hours.

D

Dark horse – a person or thing which is not the favorite to win a competition.

Down in the dumps – feeling sad; feeling blue.

E

Easy as pie – very easy.

Eat his words – admit he was wrong about something he said.

Elbow room – enough space to feel comfortable.

Elephant in the room – an embarrassing topic which everyone is aware of and no one wants to talk about.

Eyes on the prize – focused on a goal.

F

Fair weather friend – a person who is there only when the situation is easy.

Feeling blue – feeling sad for a period of some time.

Finger in a lot of pies – has many activities and projects.

Flying under the radar – trying to not be noticed.

Foot in his mouth – saying something that shouldn't have been said.

G

Gets my goat – irritates me; irks me.

Green – without experience; untested.

Green – interested in protecting nature.

Green with envy – jealous of another's possessions or
  achievements.

H

Having the inside track – having information or connections
  which are not generally known.

Hot – spicy.

Hot – popular; selling well.

Hot – sexy.

Hot hand – on a hot streak; hitting a large number of baskets in
  basketball.

Hot potato – a subject so upsetting that people try to pass it on
  to others.

Hot streak – on a roll; scoring a number of points in a row.

Hot under the collar – upset; angry.

Hotshot – a person who feels he's a star and shows it.

I

I smell a rat – I feel something is wrong; I am suspicious.

In a jam – in trouble.

In a nutshell – the main points briefly stated.

In a pickle – in trouble.

In hot water – in trouble.

In the black – making profit in a business.

In the doghouse – in trouble.

In the red – losing money in a business.

It was a walk in the park – easy.

It's a breeze – easy.

K

Kick the bucket – die.

L

Learn the ropes – learn basic information or skills.

Let the cat out of the bag – tell something which was supposed to be secret.

Let's talk turkey – talk realistically; make a deal.

Like a bull in a china shop – awkward; uncontrolled; destructive.

Like a fish out of water – feeling uncomfortable in one's situation.

N

No leg to stand on – no facts in support of one's statement.

O

Out of the blue – without a hint; a surprising occurrence.

Out of the loop – uninformed; not part of the in-group.

Out of your mind – crazy; foolish; outrageous.

Out on a limb – taking a chance; risking a prediction.

P

Pie in the sky – unrealistic; not practical.

Play it by ear – decide at the time what to do; not pre-planned; spontaneous.

Pulling my leg – teasing me.

R

Raining cats and dogs – a downpour; a very heavy rain.

S

See red – be angry.

Sell like hot cakes – be popular; be easy to sell.

Sitting on the fence – undecided.

Smells fishy – is suspicious; feels wrong.

Snow job – flattery in the hope of gaining something.

Something is fishy – feels wrong; seems suspicious.

Soup up – make something more interesting or exciting.

Spice up – make something more interesting or exciting.

Spill the beans – tell something you should not tell.

Sticks her nose in – gets in other people's personal business.

Straight from the horse's mouth - directly from an informed person

Swallow your words – admit to others that what you said was wrong.

Swallow your pride – admit to others that you were wrong.

T

Take with a grain of salt – be wary; not completely accept all that is said.

The apple of his eye – the center of his affections.

The black sheep of the family – a person whom others in the family disapprove of.

The bread winner – the main money earner in a family.

The cream of the crop – the best.

Thick skinned – not bothered by criticism.

Thin skinned – too sensitive to correction or criticism.

Tickled pink – very pleased

Toot your own horn – brag about yourself.

Treating with kid gloves – being very careful with someone.

Turns a blind eye – ignores; pretends not to see.

Turns a deaf ear – ignores; pretends not to hear.

U

Under the weather – not feeling as well as usual.

Underdog – a competitor who is not expected to win.

Up in the air – undecided

Up the creek – in a hard situation; having problems.

Up the creek without a paddle – in a difficult situation; having problems.

W

Walking on eggshells – being very careful around someone.
Wet behind the ears – inexperienced.

ANSWER KEY

UNIT 1: LET'S GET STARTED

Lesson 1: It's a Breeze

Practice 1: cashier, sack, breeze

Lesson 2: Learn the Ropes

Practice 1: tip, restaurant, salary

Lesson 3: Toot Your Own Horn

Practice 2: boxer, uncomfortable, toot

Lesson 4: Bucket List

Practice 1: Statue of Liberty, bucket, dream

UNIT 2: FOOD IDIOMS

Lesson 5: A Piece of Cake

Practice 1: prepare, upcoming, interview

Lesson 6: In a Pickle

Practice 1: traveling salesman, furious, pickle

Practice 2: yes, no, no, yes

Lesson 7: A Peach

Practice 1: rare, wonderful, pets

Lesson 8: Eat His Words

Practice 1: bonus, final, compete

Lesson 9: Something Is Fishy

Practice 1: contract, suspicious, economy

Practice 2: yes, yes, yes

Lesson 10: Couch Potato

Practice 1: glued, sluggish, couch

Lesson 11: Walking on Eggshells

Practice 1: tense, unpleasantness, tease

Lesson 12: Pie in the Sky

Practice 1: assignments, counselor, unrealistic

REVIEW OF UNIT 2: FOOD IDIOMS

Matching: 1E, 2C, 3D, 4B, 5A, 6F

UNIT 3: BODY LANGUAGE

Lesson 13: A Pain in the Neck

Practice 1: neighbor, strict, pest

Practice 2: father-in-law, brother-in-law, sister-in-law, daughter-in-law, son-in-law.

Lesson 14: Pulling My Leg

Practice 1: lottery, tricks, serious

Lesson 15: Turns a Blind Eye

Practice 1: manager, blind, diamond

Practice 2: yes, yes, no, yes

Lesson 16: Wet Behind the Ears

Practice 1: wages, suburbs, minimum

Lesson 17: Thin Skinned

Practice 1: lawyer, correction, retired

Practice 2: yes, no, no, no, yes

Lesson 18: Out of Your Mind

Practice 1: mall, price, bored

REVIEW OF UNIT 3: BODY BUILDING

Matching: 1E, 2G, 3B, 4A, 5H, 6C, 7D, 8F, 9I

Lesson 30: Tickled Pink

Practice 1: local, future, apartment

DO YOU KNOW YOUR COLORS?

pink, black, red, black, red, purple, white, blue, pink, green, green

REVIEW OF UNIT 5: COLORFUL COMMENTS

Matching: 1C, 2F, 3A, 4B, 5D, 6E

UNIT 6: HOW'S THE WEATHER?

Lesson 31: Under the Weather

Practice 1: yesterday, crisis, cheerful

Lesson 32: Raining Cats and Dogs

Practice 1: legal, soaked, free

Practice 2: something, handbag, raincoat, somewhere, basketball, pancake, snowball, dollhouse, eyeglasses, washrag, earring, fingernail

Lesson 33: Fair Weather Friend

Practice 1: chatting, fatal, betrayed

Lesson 34: Chill Out/Be Cool

Practice 1: relax, furious, shift

Lesson 35: In Hot Water

Practice 1: play, noisy, buddies

REVIEW OF UNIT 6: WEATHER REPORT

Matching: 1F, 2G, 3A, 4E, 5C, 6D, 7B

UNIT 7: WHERE ARE YOU?

Lesson 36: Sitting on the Fence

Practice 1: fence, committed, election

Lesson 37: Out on a Limb

Practice 2: record, limb, risk

Lesson 38: Up in the Air

Practice 1: grounded, vague, vision

Lesson 39: Down in the Dumps

Practice 1: hospital, ruined, stadium

Lesson 40: Between a Rock and a Hard Place

Practice 1: citizen, option, trapped

Lesson 41: Out of the Loop

Practice 1: memo, division, executive

Practice 2: gym, phone, TV or tele, auto, bike

Lesson 42: Flying Under the Radar

Practice 1: radar, director, attention

UNIT 7 REVIEW: WHERE ARE YOU?

Matching: 1E, 2G, 3C, 4B, 5D, 6A, 7F

FINAL REVIEW: DO YOU REALLY KNOW YOUR IDIOMS?

Matching: 1B, 2E, 3F, 4D, 5G, 6H, 7I, 8J, 9K, 10L, 11M, 12N, 13O, 14C, 15A

ABOUT THE AUTHOR

TONI ABERSON has written educational books since retiring from teaching English to high school and college students and supervising high school English teachers for 35 years. Aberson (M.A. English; M.A. Psychology and Religion) believes that a lively classroom is the optimal learning environment.

"If people are thinking, sharing, and laughing, then they're learning," notes Aberson, the co-author of *Compelling American Conversations: Questions and Quotations for Intermediate English Language Learners*. "The mere fact that students are in an English classroom attests to their courage and their determination to learn."

"Both high school and adult English students bring a wealth of interesting experiences with them," continues Aberson. "They bring the world into the classroom. The challenge for English teachers is to put students at ease and encourage them to practice English. What better way than to ask students about their lives? I love teaching English."

Aberson has co-authored two additional Chimayo Press books for adult English language learners. Her first book, *Compelling Conversations: Questions and Quotations on Timeless Topics*, a fluency-focused advanced English as Second Language (ESL) textbook, has been used by English learners, teachers, and tutors in over 50 countries. *It's A Breeze: 42 Lively English Lessons on American Idioms* reflects her focus on real-life expressions and situations—and the importance of authentic communication for teenagers, college students, and working adults.

"The key in a classroom is engagement," notes Aberson, a member of Teachers of English to Speakers of Other Languages (TESOL). "People become interested and excited when they're learning about the daily stuff of life. When students are thinking and writing and talking about their real lives—food, jobs, family, homes, sports, movies—that's when students learn the language."

"Learning English is not easy," continues Aberson. "It can be a real challenge, but it can also be fun and stimulating. That's what I'm aiming for—the real life and the fun that stimulates ESL students so they want to learn more and share their experiences. Everybody wants to jump in, and earning English becomes a breeze."

Aberson lives in Southern California, where she loves to garden and spend as much time as possible on the beach.

ERIC H. ROTH (editor) teaches international students the pleasures of writing and speaking English at the University of Southern California. For the last twenty years, he has taught English to high school, community college, and university students. Roth co-authored the *Compelling Conversations* series of fluency-focused ESL textbooks with Aberson, and has taught in France, Spain, and Vietnam. He has also given CATESOL and TESOL presentations on effective communicative teaching methods. *It's A Breeze* is his fourth Chimayo Press publication.

ABOUT THIS BOOK AND CHIMAYO PRESS

It's A Breeze: 42 Lively English Lessons on American Idioms explicitly emphasizes American phrases in short, self-contained lessons.

The primary audience is newcomers to the United States as well as recent and not-so-recent immigrants, who may be studying at an American high school, adult school, community college, or university. Speaking English remains the passport to a better life, and understanding and using American idioms remains essential to clearly communicate with native speakers. Unfortunately, idioms are often confusing and usually only taught at the most advanced levels. Many lower level English language learners often find idioms particularly difficult. This thin volume clearly introduces common American idioms in a comfortable manner with short reading, writing, and speaking exercises.

Intended as a supplemental textbook for beginning high or intermediate low English language learners, *It's A Breeze* can add a vital linguistic element to traditional life skills curriculum for high school, adult, and community college classes. English teachers and private tutors can also use the book as a textbook for the rare idioms class. Literacy programs and Intensive English programs can use it as a high-low text for their students.

All immigrants deserve a quality education that allows them to express themselves, develop their English language skills, and deepen their critical thinking skills. Classrooms can also provide sanctuary for sometimes isolated, often stressed students. This book provides students the words and phrases to share their experiences in vivid English. It also attempts to fill in common gaps between student interests and the sometimes narrow focus of standardized tests.

Chimayo Press, an independent publishing company, believes that many language programs too often teach students to mostly listen and seldom speak—and often underestimate the academic, social, and professional abilities of many American immigrants.

Therefore, we deliberately chose to emphasize speaking skills and fluency in all of our books for English language learners. Our first book, *Compelling Conversations: Questions and Quotations on Timeless Topics* has been used in English classrooms in over 50 countries. Since 2007, Chimayo Press has created quality niche books. The series continued with *Compelling American Conversations: Questions and Quotations for Intermediate American English Language Learners* in 2012. *It's A Breeze* is our fourth title.

All Chimayo Press titles include both practical topics and philosophical questions because American immigrants deserve the same level of sophisticated materials that international English as Foreign Language (EFL) students enjoy in the stronger international schools. We hope American English language learners begin asking more questions, speak more in their workplaces, and create their own compelling conversations — across the globe.

Visit us at www.ChimayoPress.com to find more tips on fluently speaking English, to suggest conversation topics, or to contribute your favorite proverbs and quotations.

1-855-ESL-Book (toll free)
1-855-375-2665